SMART SKETCH BOOK

Oogie Art's step-by-step guide to drawing basic human joints in charcoal and pastel.

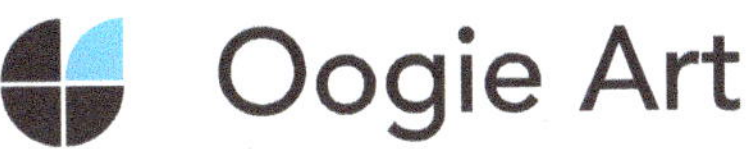

Oogie Art's SmartSketchbook™
An Expert's Guide to Joints in Charcoal, Pastel and Acrylic
First Edition, Copyright © 2015

Produced and Edited by
Oogie Art
New York, NY

© Text
Oogie Art

© Photographs
Licensed under Oogie Art®

Directed by
Wook Choi

Assistant Directed by
Clara Lu

Drawings by
Jee Hwang

Tips by
Wook Choi

Published and Distributed by
Oogie Publishing House
New York, NY
www.oogiepublishinghouse.com
(212) 714-1011

ISBN 978-0-9855809-7-1
Printed in the United States

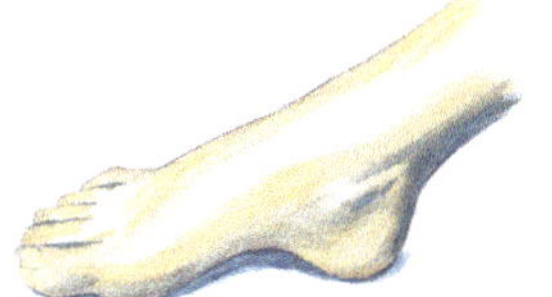
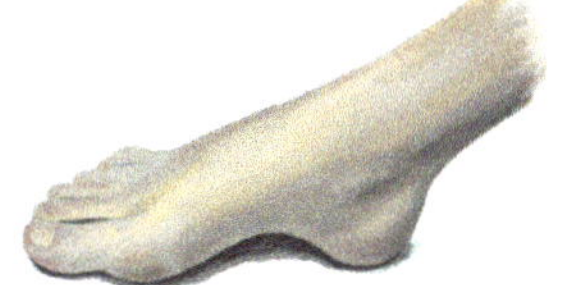
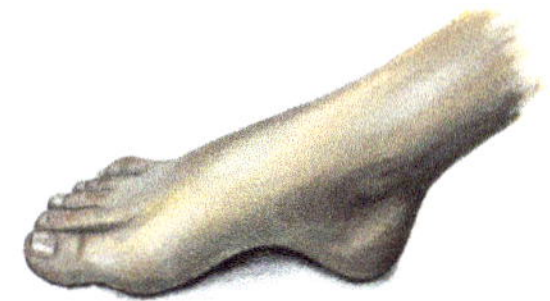

CONTENTS

Introduction to Anatomy of Joints 4
Types of Joints 5
General Hand Anatomy 6
Hand in Charcoal 8
Hands in Pastel 12
Hands in Acrylic 16
General Hand Positions 20
General Foot Anatomy 22
Foot in Charcoal 24
Foot in Pastel 28
Foot in Acrylic 32
General Foot Positions 36
General Knee Anatomy 38
Knee in Charcoal 40
Knee in Pastel 44
General Knee Positions 48
General Elbow Anatomy 50
Elbow in Charcoal 52
Elbow in Pastel 56
General Elbow Positions 60

Introduction to Joints

A joint is where bones connect, which gives us basic movement, and are a very important part of portraying body language when drawing the figure. There are many joints in your body. Hands, feet, elbows, and knees are just a few places that are predominately joints.

Study the different types of joints in the body on the next page in order to render more accurate positions of the body.

What you'll need

- Brushes (an assortment Bright and Round brushes in varying sizes), refer to page 6 for guidance
- Acrylic Paints in varying colors
- Paper Palette
- Palette Knife
- Canvas

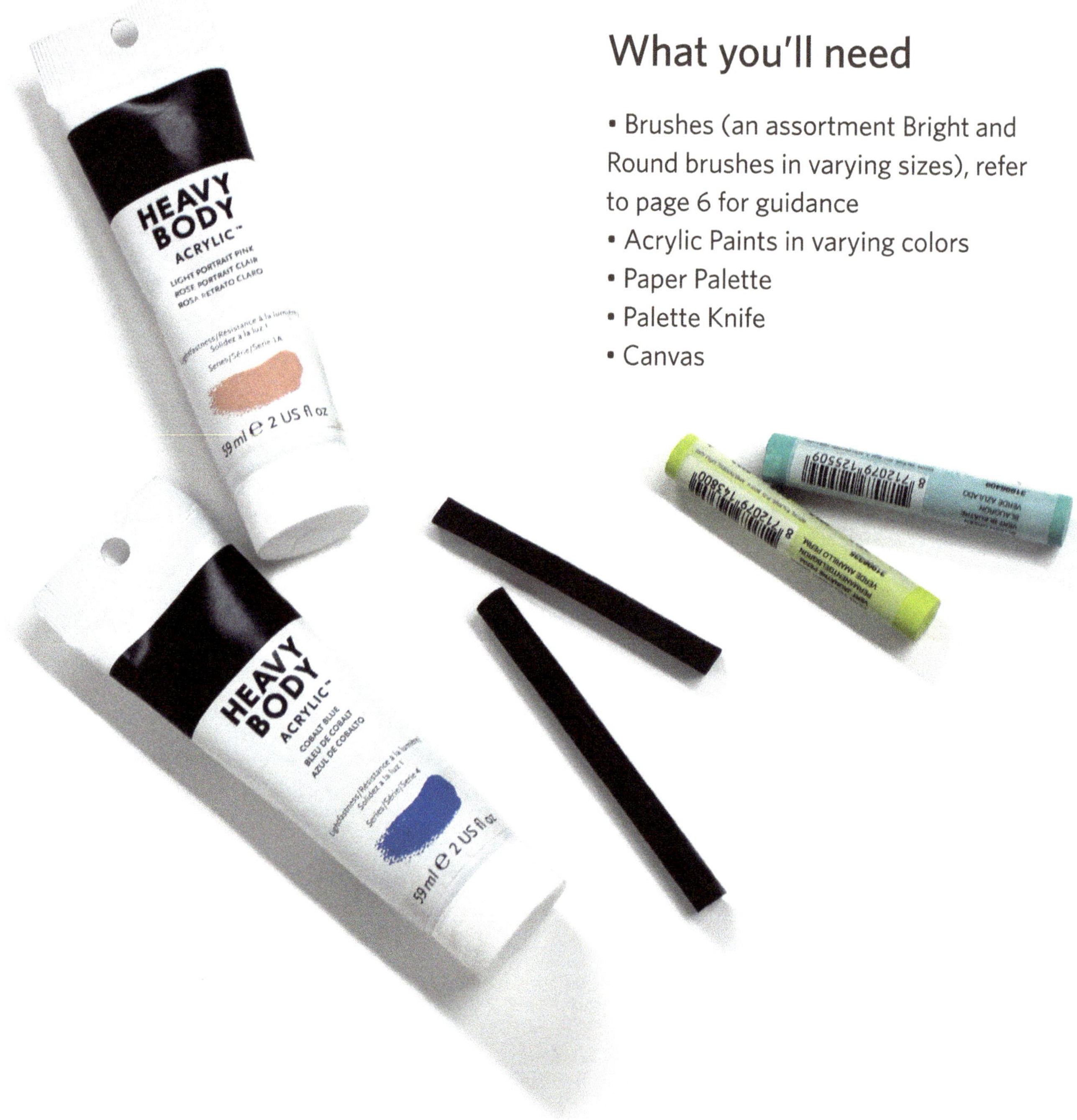

Types of Joints

The key to drawing successful joints is making sure the angles they are forming are correct. Another important aspect to pay attention to is proportion: make sure that each segment of the joint is proportional to the other. A basic understanding of how all the bones and muscles work under the skin will help greatly in creating realistic-looking hands and limbs.

Hinge Joints

The most common joint allowing for one directional movement. Examples of these are the elbow and knee joints.

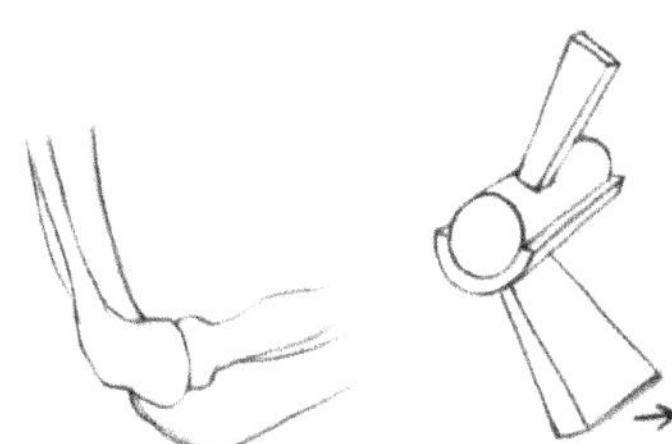

Gliding Joints

These joints allow sliding movement in any direction. Many gliding joints are found in the hands and wrist.

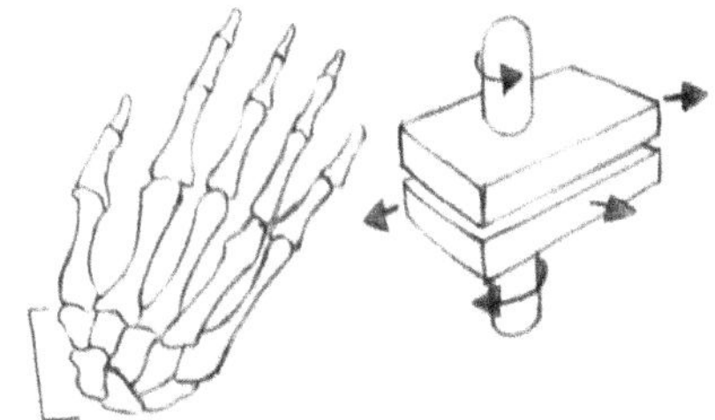

Saddle Joints

These joints allow for biaxial movements (front to back and side to side). An example of this is the joint connecting the thumb to the wrist.

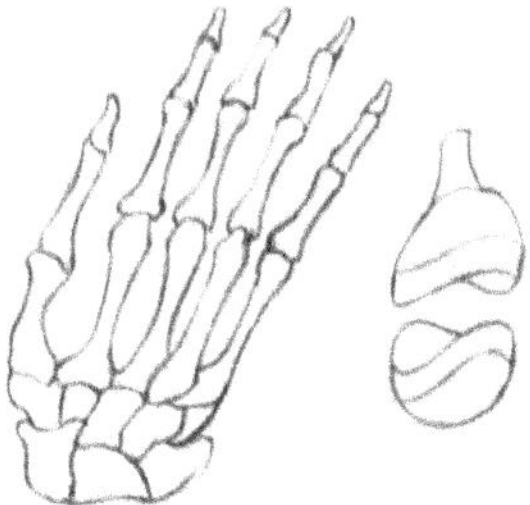

Ball and Socket Joints

Ball and Socket joints allow for full circular motion. The shoulder and hip joints are the only ball and socket joints in the body.

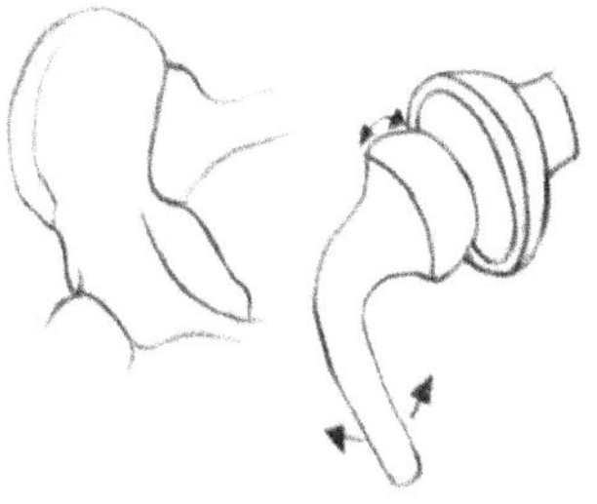

Hands can be confusing to draw, given the number of joints, but here is where knowledge of the proportions and angles of the hand come into play. First, you can break the hand down into simpler structures. The palm of the hand forms a soft rectangular shape. The fingers branch off and are roughly the same length of the palm, if a little shorter. Simplify the fingers as three stacked cylinders. This will help determine shading later on.

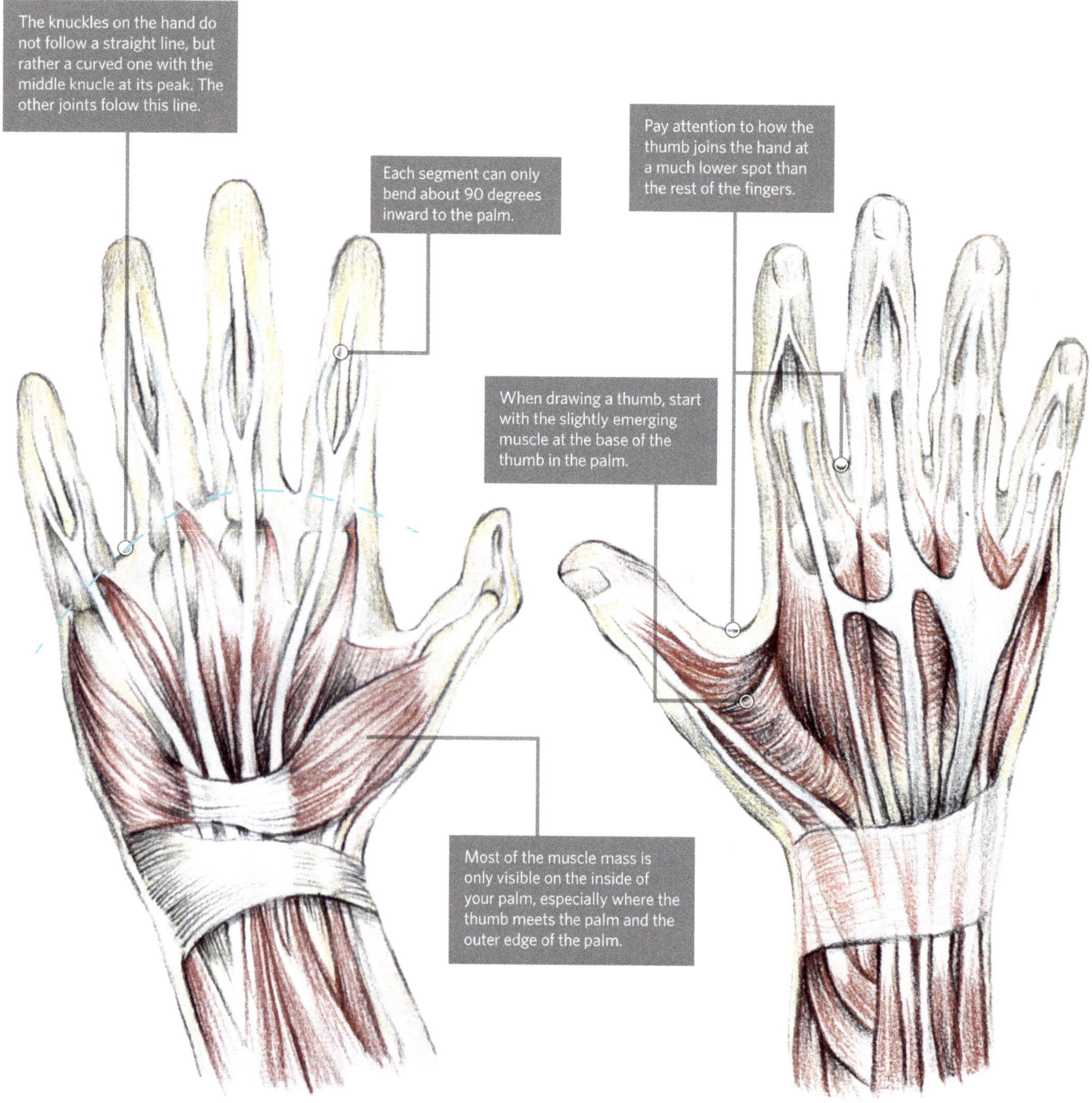

PRACTICE

Now try drawing the hand structure yourself.

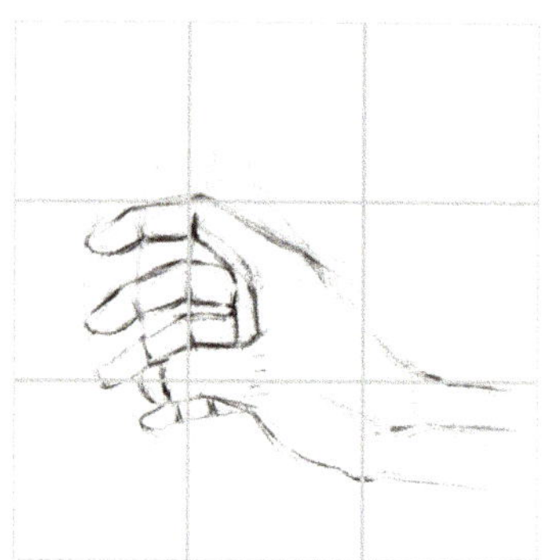

Draw the general lines to describe the shape of the hand, using guidelines to help you draw the position of the fingers.

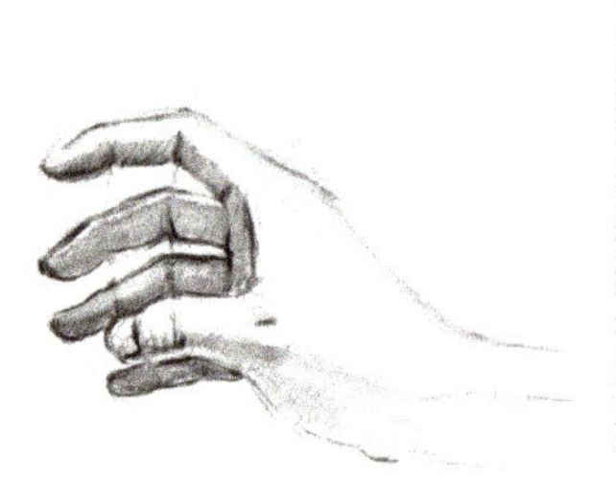

Shade in the general areas of shadow. Notice how the interior of the hand is darker because it is facing away from the light source.

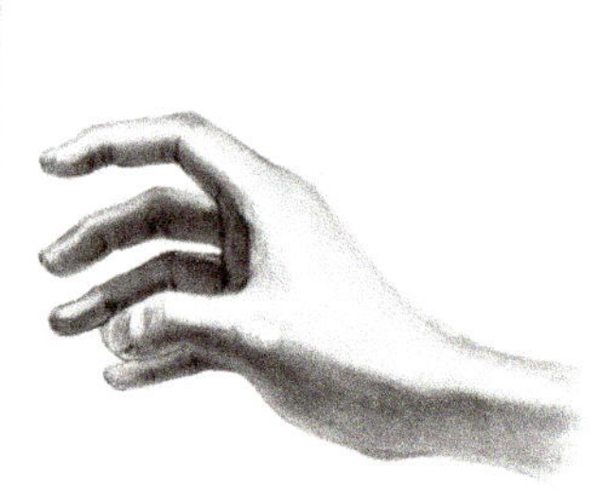

Begin to further define the shadows and smooth them out to create more of a skin-like appearance. Connect the shadow through the bottom of the palm and the arm.

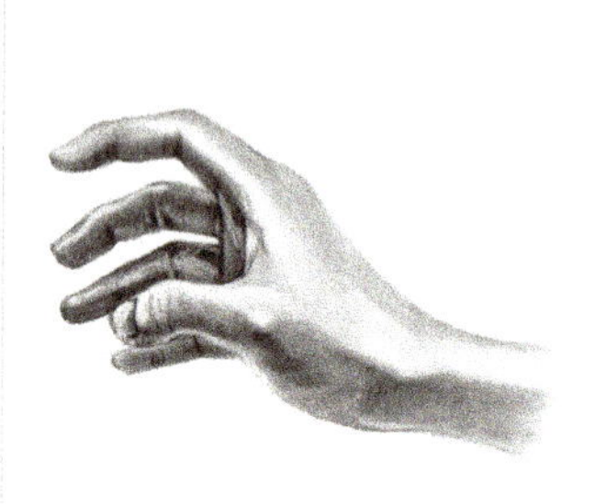

Continue to render skin tones, details, and wrinkles as well as textures of the hand using a little bit of compressed charcoal and mostly vine charcoal.

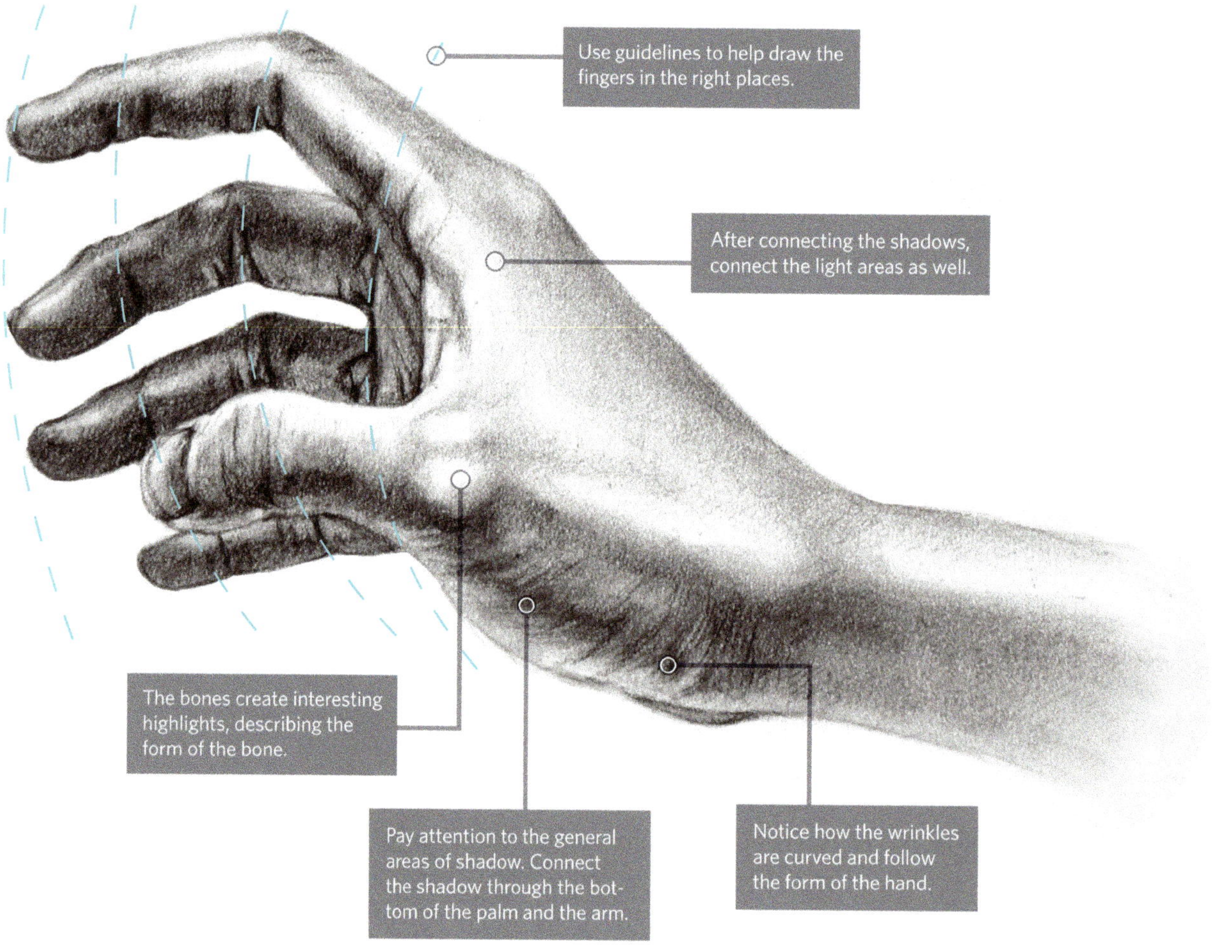

Use guidelines to help draw the fingers in the right places.

After connecting the shadows, connect the light areas as well.

The bones create interesting highlights, describing the form of the bone.

Pay attention to the general areas of shadow. Connect the shadow through the bottom of the palm and the arm.

Notice how the wrinkles are curved and follow the form of the hand.

Now try drawing the hand yourself.

Now that you have practiced how to draw a hand in charcoal following a step-by-step tutorial, use the page on the right to try and draw from life. You can draw from the picture below, use a mirror, or ask a friend to sit for you and try different variations of compositions.

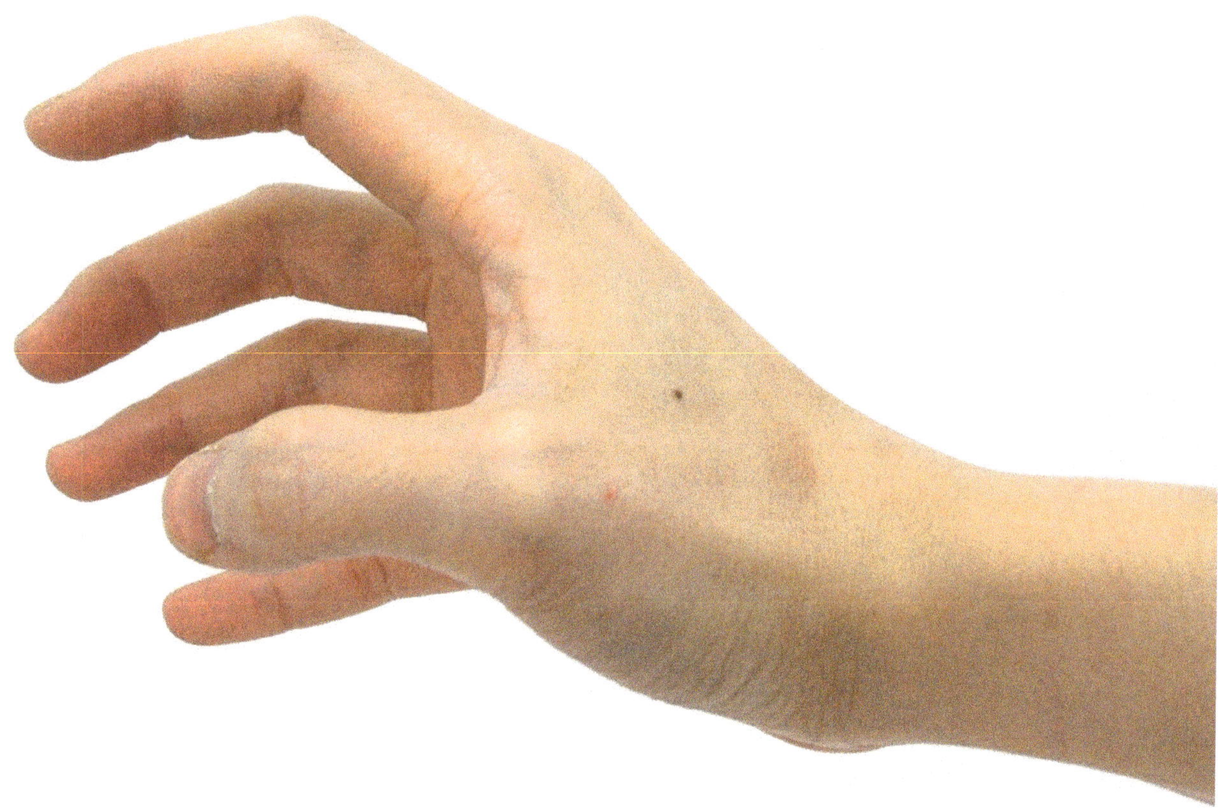

Now try drawing the hand yourself without the grid.

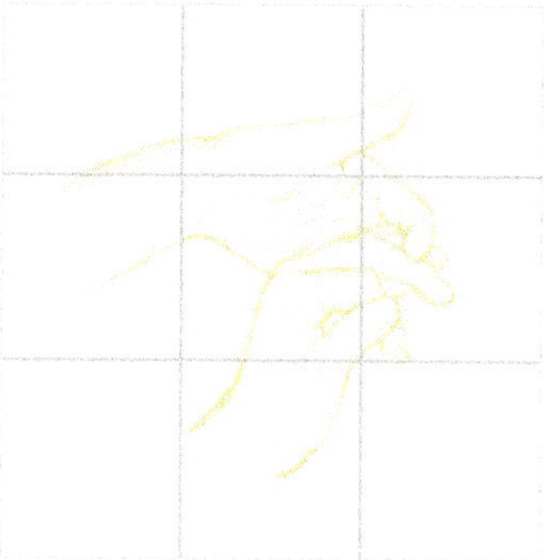

Create guidelines to describe the shape of the two left hands using yellow. Draw the two hands, the general outlines first.

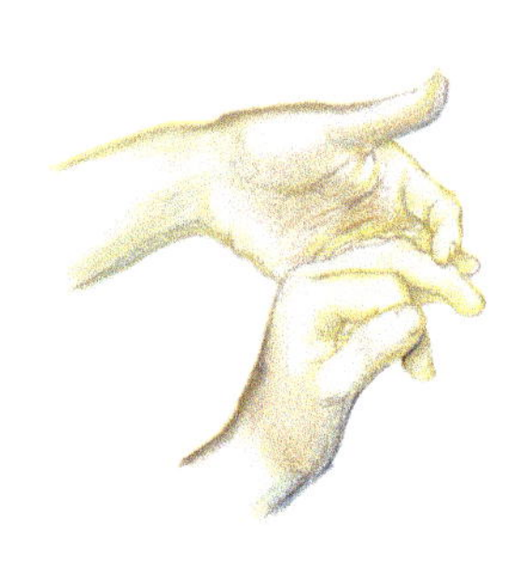

Try to draw and shade the hands together, not one by one, so as to continue to see the relationship of lights and darks better.

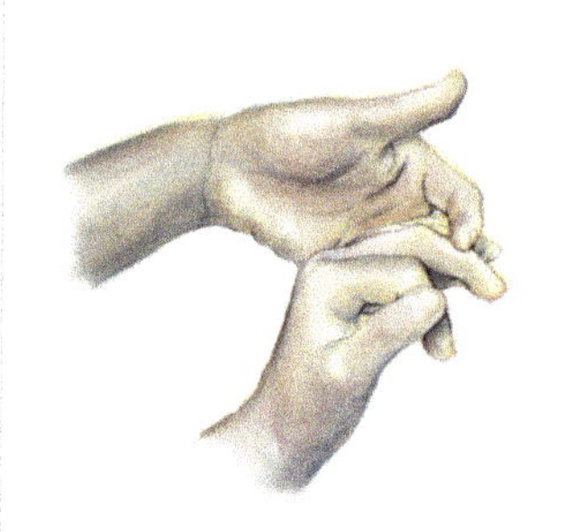

Using like skin tones such as pinks, yellows, light browns and purples, render the general volume of the hands.

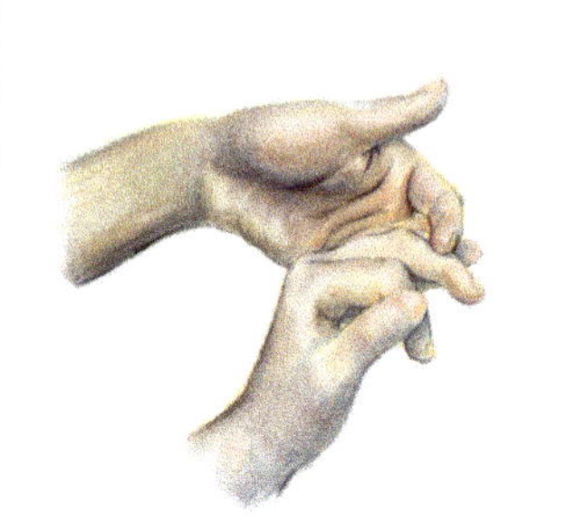

Continue to add layers of colors to render volume and begin to add in the general wrinkle details of the hands. Pay attention to where the light is coming from.

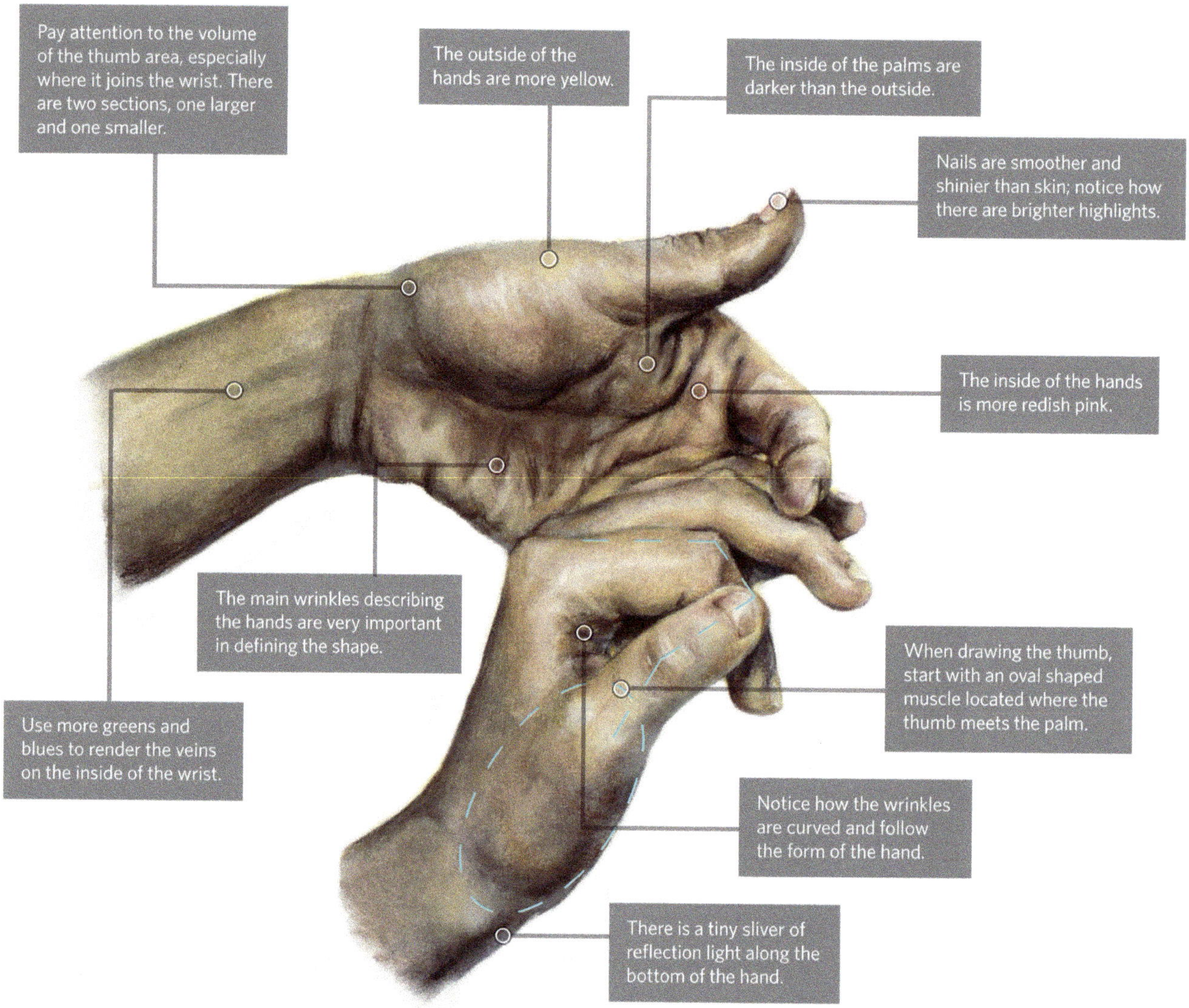

Pay attention to the volume of the thumb area, especially where it joins the wrist. There are two sections, one larger and one smaller.

The outside of the hands are more yellow.

The inside of the palms are darker than the outside.

Nails are smoother and shinier than skin; notice how there are brighter highlights.

The inside of the hands is more redish pink.

The main wrinkles describing the hands are very important in defining the shape.

Use more greens and blues to render the veins on the inside of the wrist.

When drawing the thumb, start with an oval shaped muscle located where the thumb meets the palm.

Notice how the wrinkles are curved and follow the form of the hand.

There is a tiny sliver of reflection light along the bottom of the hand.

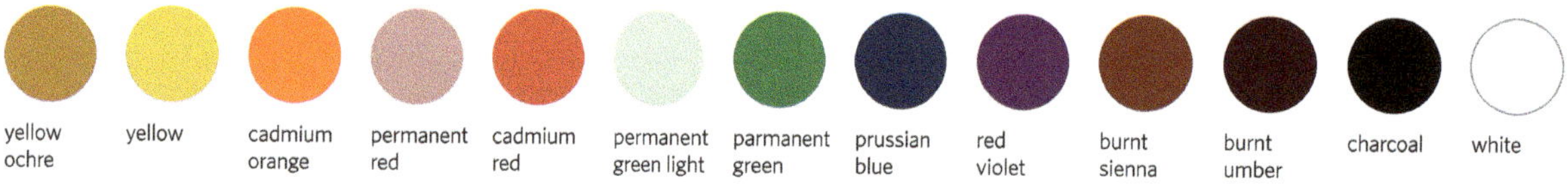

yellow ochre | yellow | cadmium orange | permanent red | cadmium red | permanent green light | parmanent green | prussian blue | red violet | burnt sienna | burnt umber | charcoal | white

Now try drawing the hands yourself.

Now that you have practiced how to draw two left hands in pastel following a step-by-step tutorial, use the page on the right to try and draw from life. You can draw from the picture below, use a mirror, or ask a friend to sit for you and try different variations of compositions.

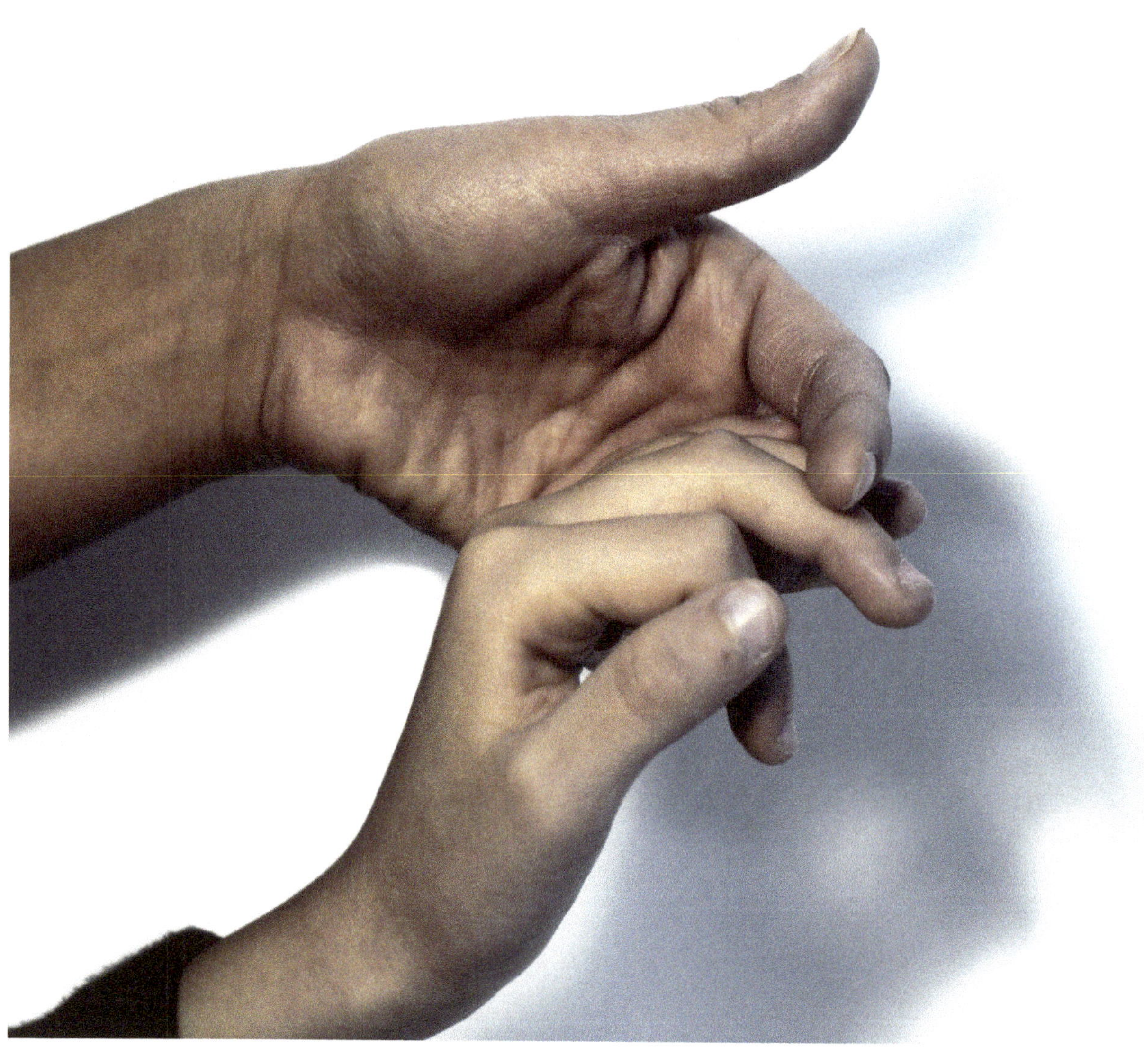

Now try drawing the hands yourself without the grid.

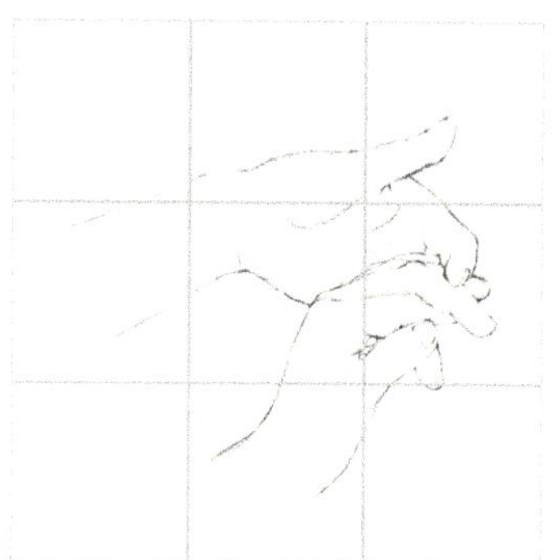

Create guidelines to describe the shape of the two left hands using pencil. Draw the two hands, the general outlines first.

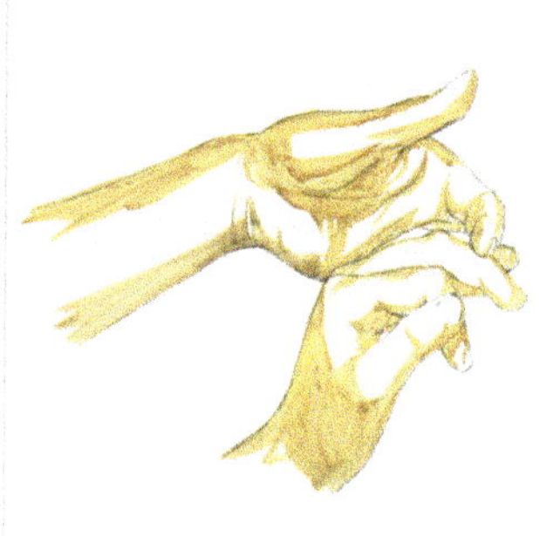

Begin blocking in the general areas of shadow using yellow ochre paint.

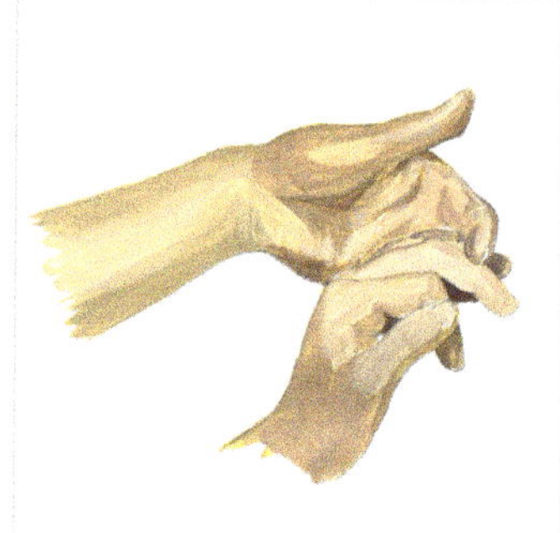

Then add in all the midtones, paying more attention to the values of the shadows and lights.

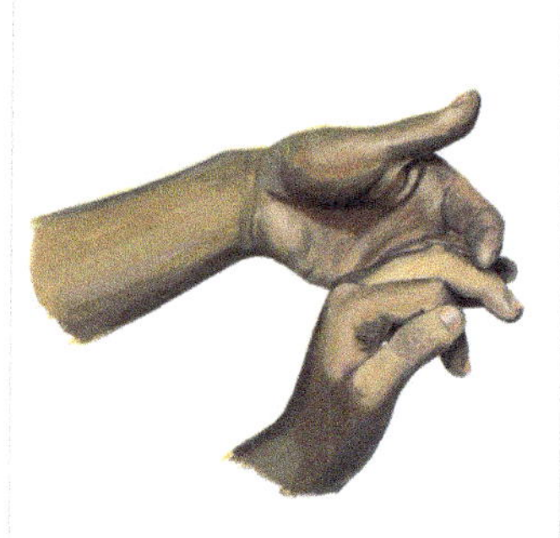

Continue to render the volume mixing yellows, oranges, reds, pinks, blues, and greens to create more rich skin tones.

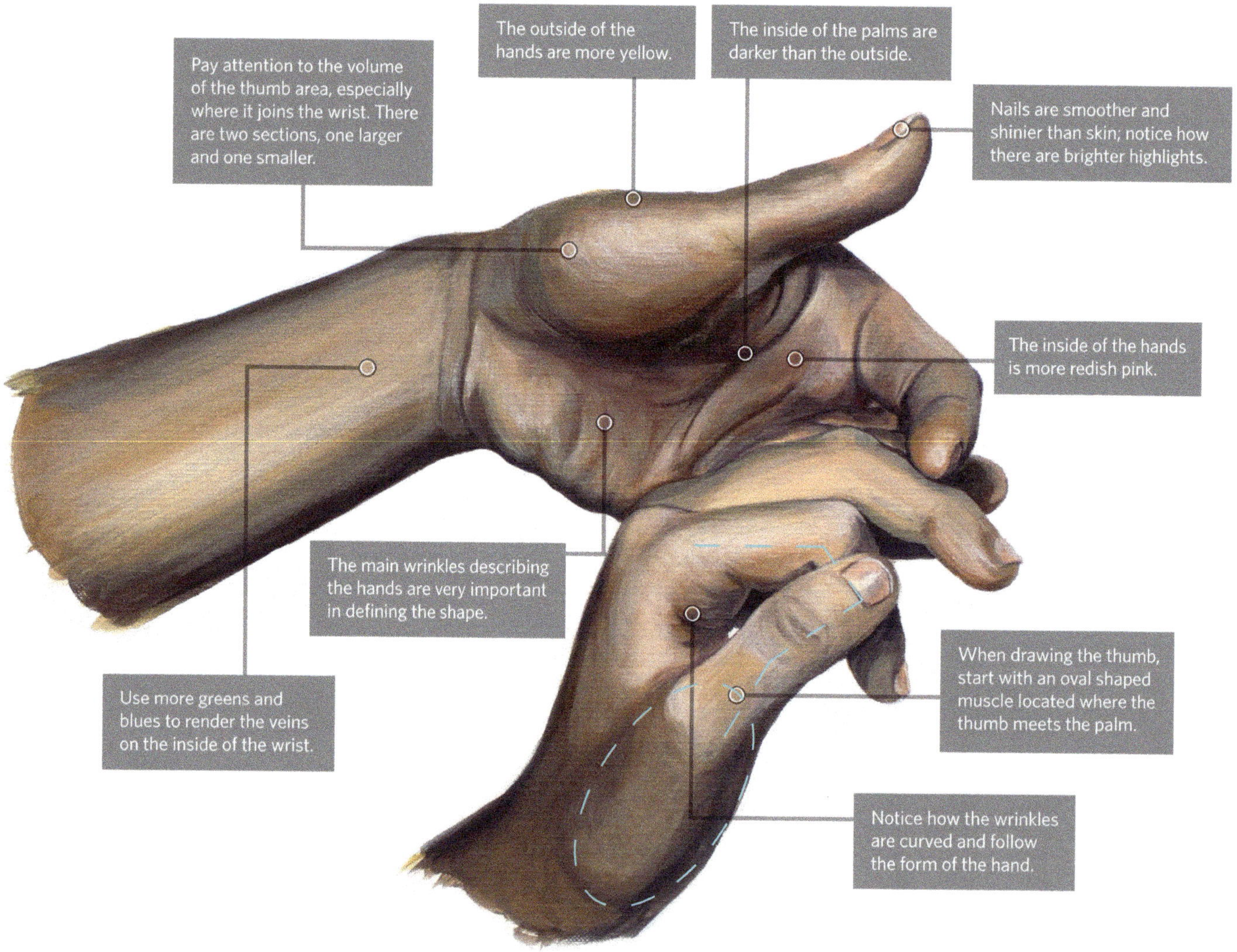

Pay attention to the volume of the thumb area, especially where it joins the wrist. There are two sections, one larger and one smaller.

The outside of the hands are more yellow.

The inside of the palms are darker than the outside.

Nails are smoother and shinier than skin; notice how there are brighter highlights.

The inside of the hands is more redish pink.

The main wrinkles describing the hands are very important in defining the shape.

Use more greens and blues to render the veins on the inside of the wrist.

When drawing the thumb, start with an oval shaped muscle located where the thumb meets the palm.

Notice how the wrinkles are curved and follow the form of the hand.

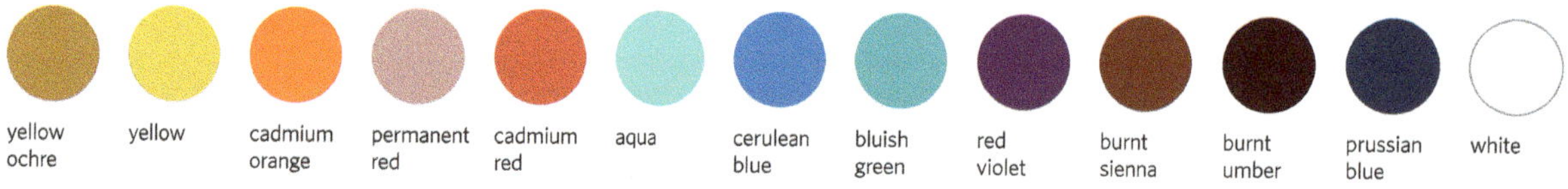

yellow ochre, yellow, cadmium orange, permanent red, cadmium red, aqua, cerulean blue, bluish green, red violet, burnt sienna, burnt umber, prussian blue, white

Now try painting the hands yourself.

Now that you have practiced how to paint two left hands in acrylic following a step-by-step tutorial, use the page on the right to try and paint from life. You can paint from the picture below, use a mirror, or ask a friend to sit for you and try different variations of compositions.

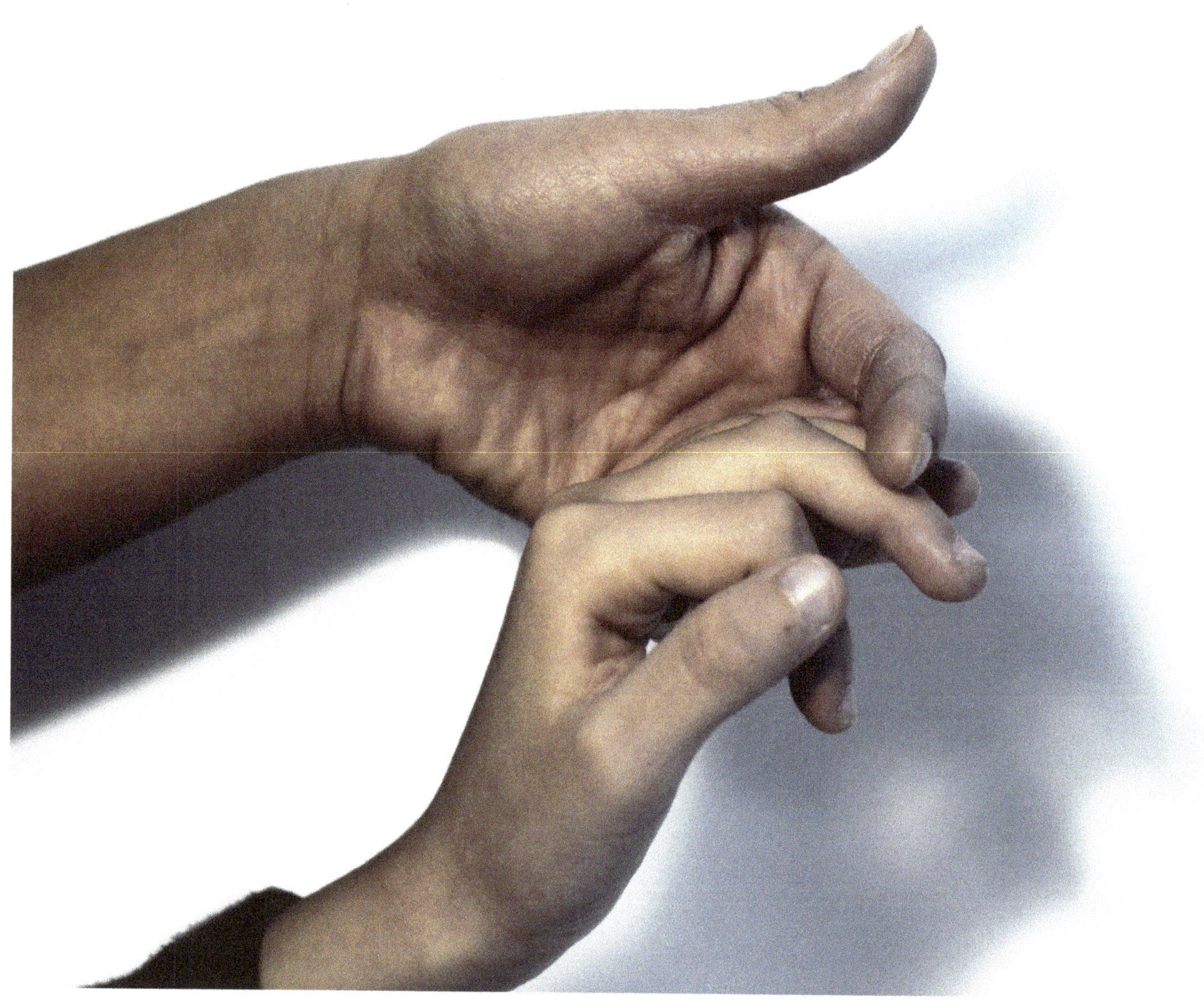

HAND IN ACRYLIC: PRACTICE II

Now try painting the hand yourself without the grid.

Now that you have practiced how to draw hands in charcoal and pastel following step-by-step tutorials, use the page on the right to try and draw from life. You can draw from the picture below, use a mirror, or ask a friend to sit for you and try different variations of perspectives to help better your understanding of the structure of the hand.

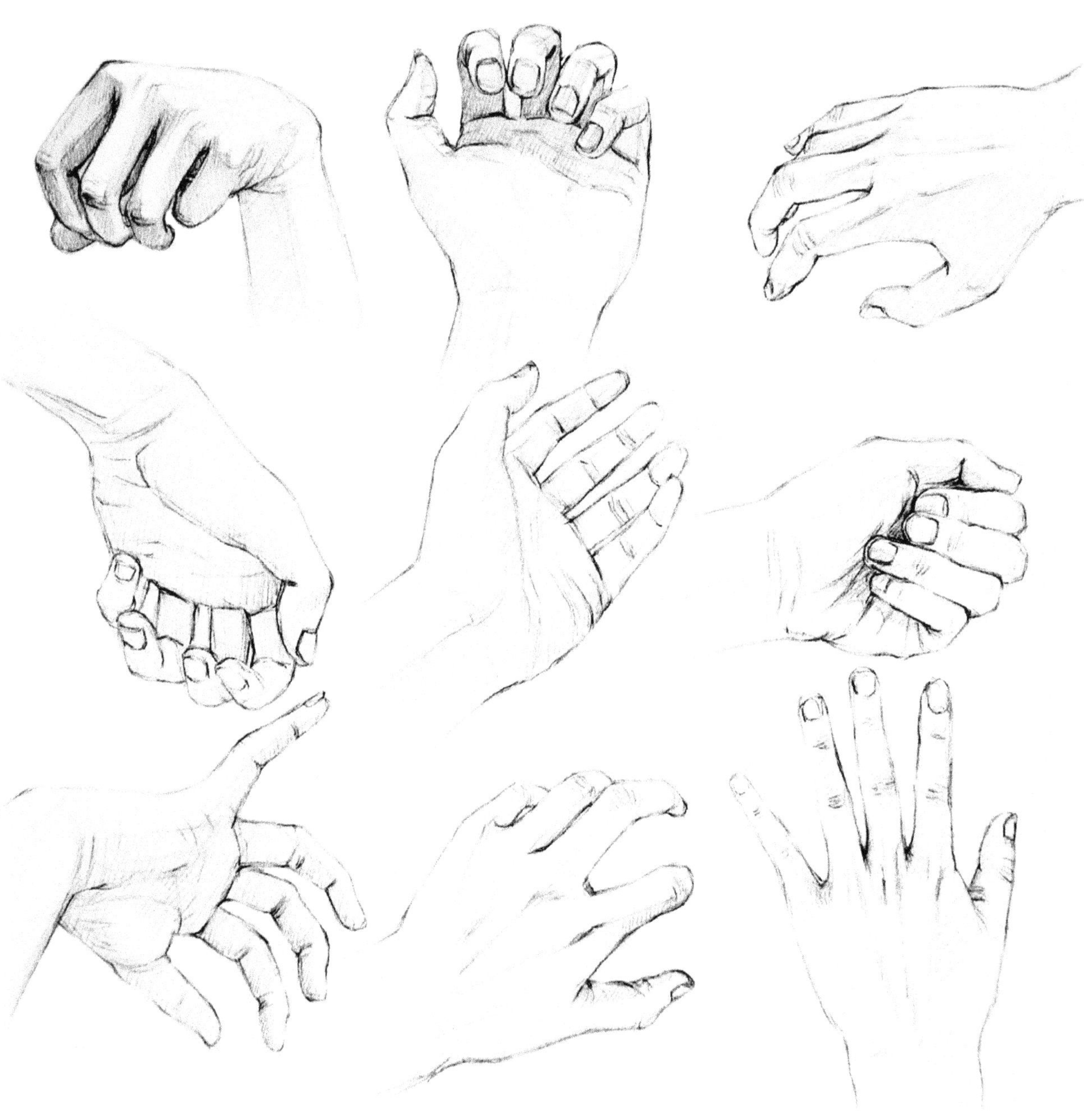

Now try drawing the hand positions yourself.

The bones in your foot are designed to carry your whole weight and more, giving your feet a stocky and solid look. There are two major arches in your foot, giving shape to the bottom and top. The first arch is the large one under the foot toward the inside. The top arch gives your foot a wedge shape.

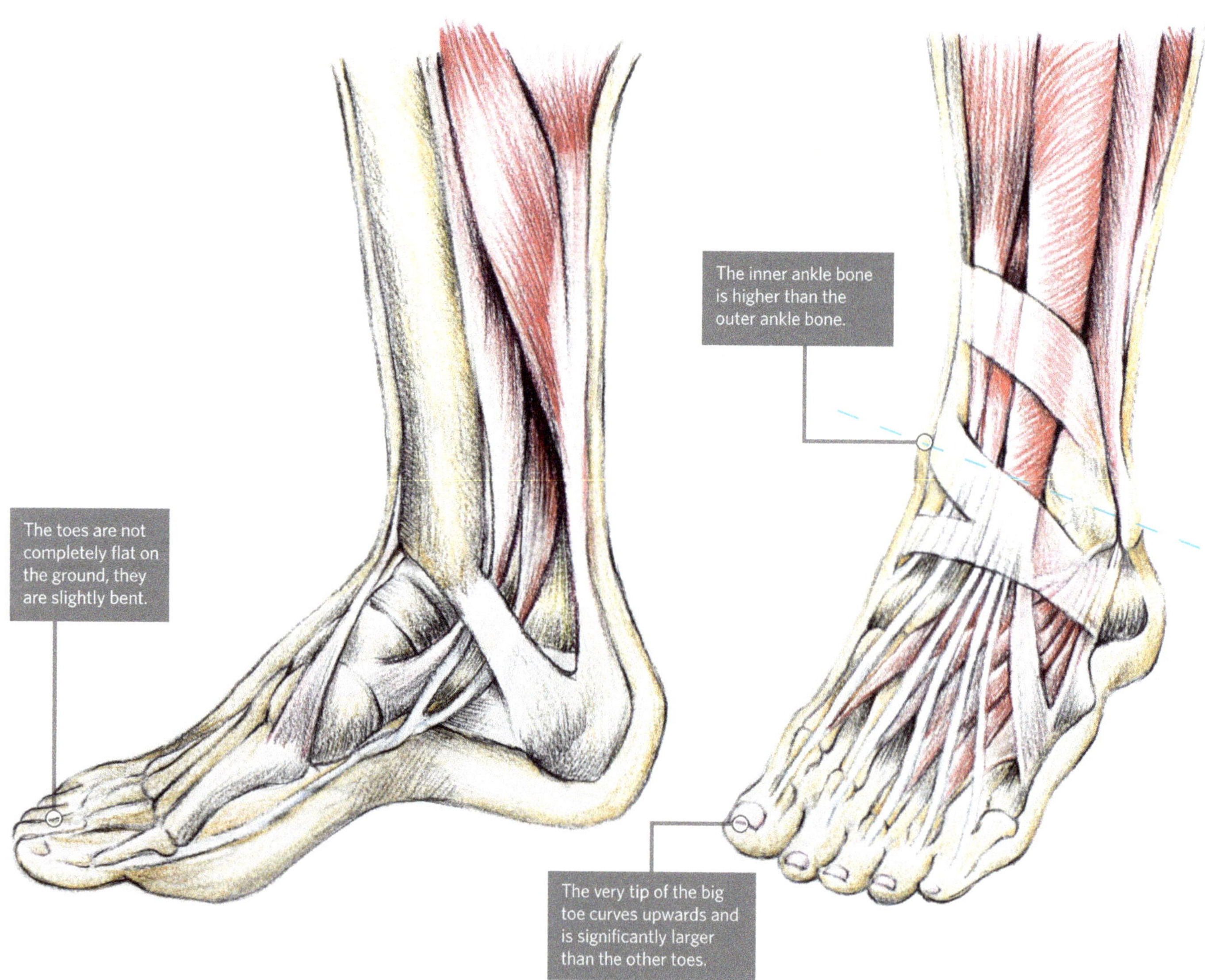

PRACTICE

Now try drawing the feet structure yourself.

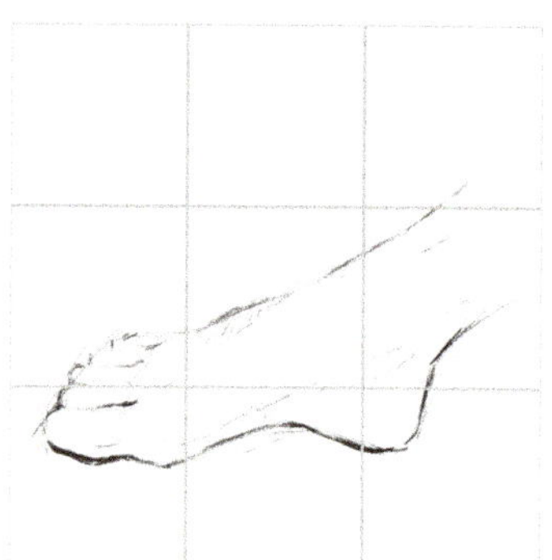
Begin by lightly creating an outline of the foot in vine charcoal.

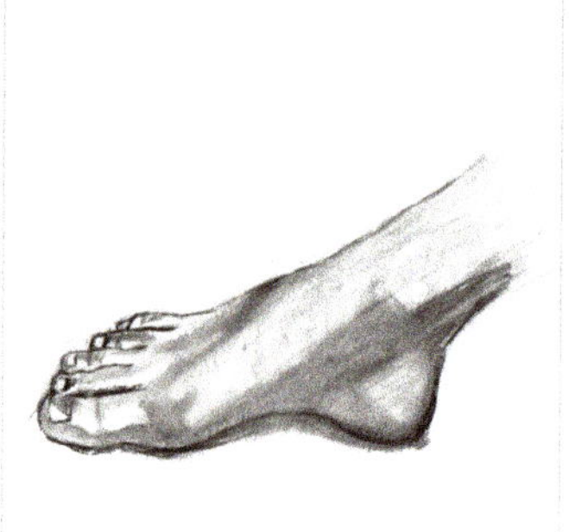
Block in the general areas of shadow and light on the foot.

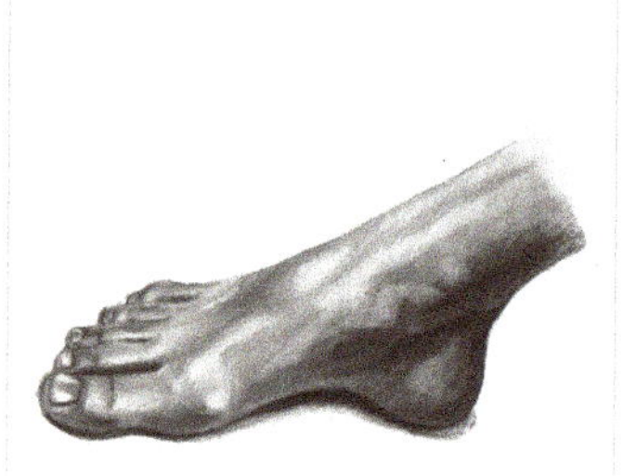
Continue to render the volume of the foot by introducing compressed charcoal.

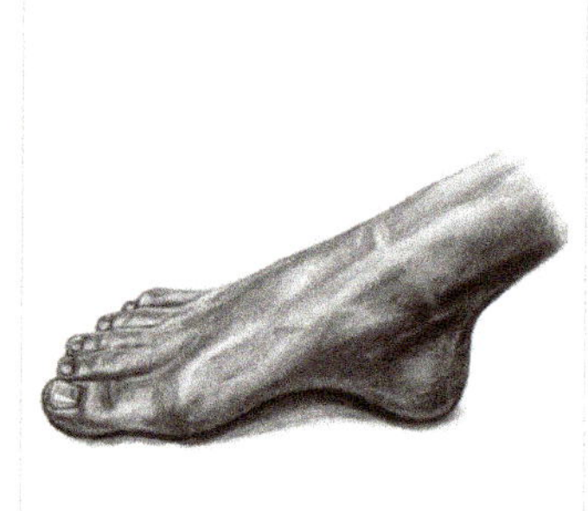
Continue to render the volume of the foot, paying attention to the general geometric shape of the foot and how light hits the foot.

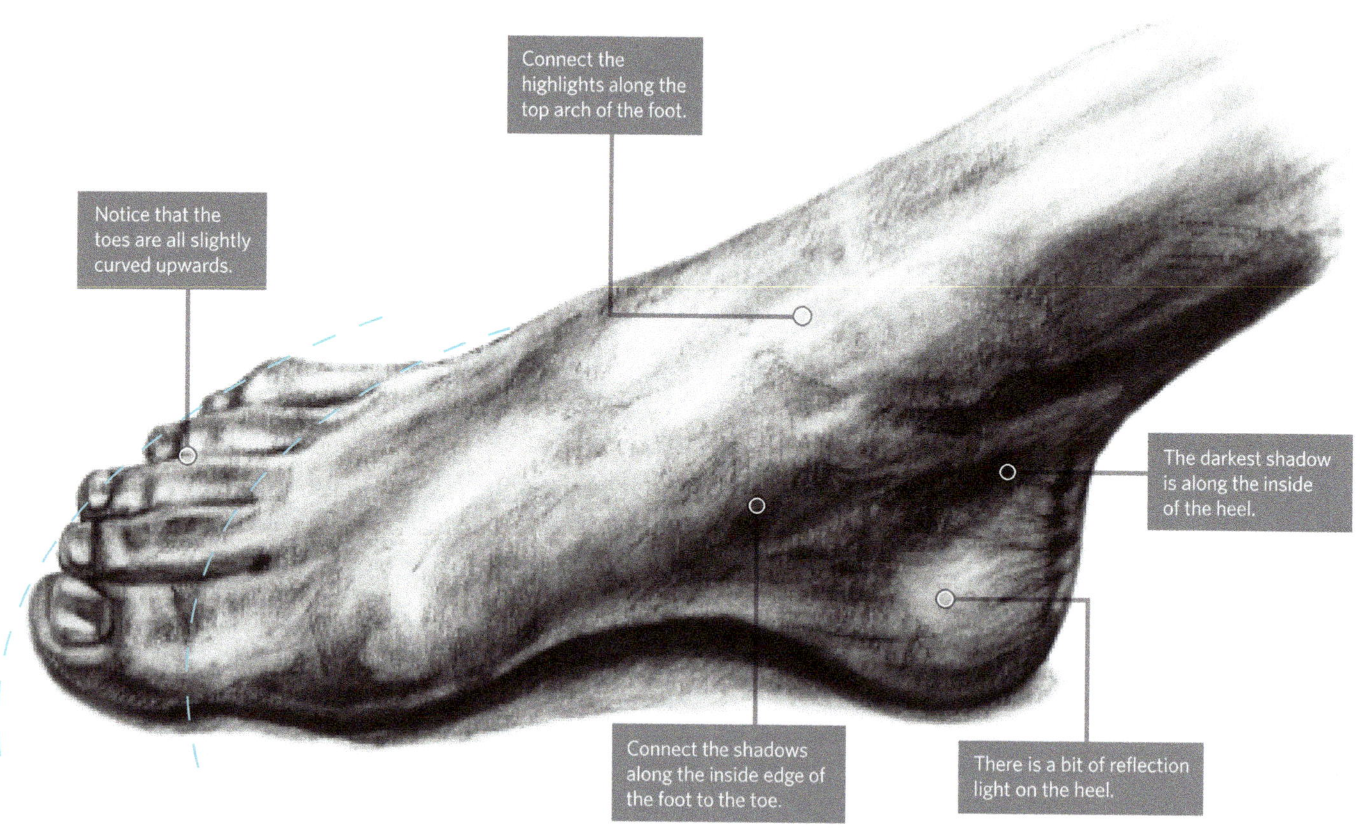

Now try drawing the foot yourself.

Now that you have practiced how to draw a right foot in charcoal following a step-by-step tutorial, use the page on the right to try and draw from life. You can draw from the picture below, use a mirror, or ask a friend to sit for you and try different variations of compositions.

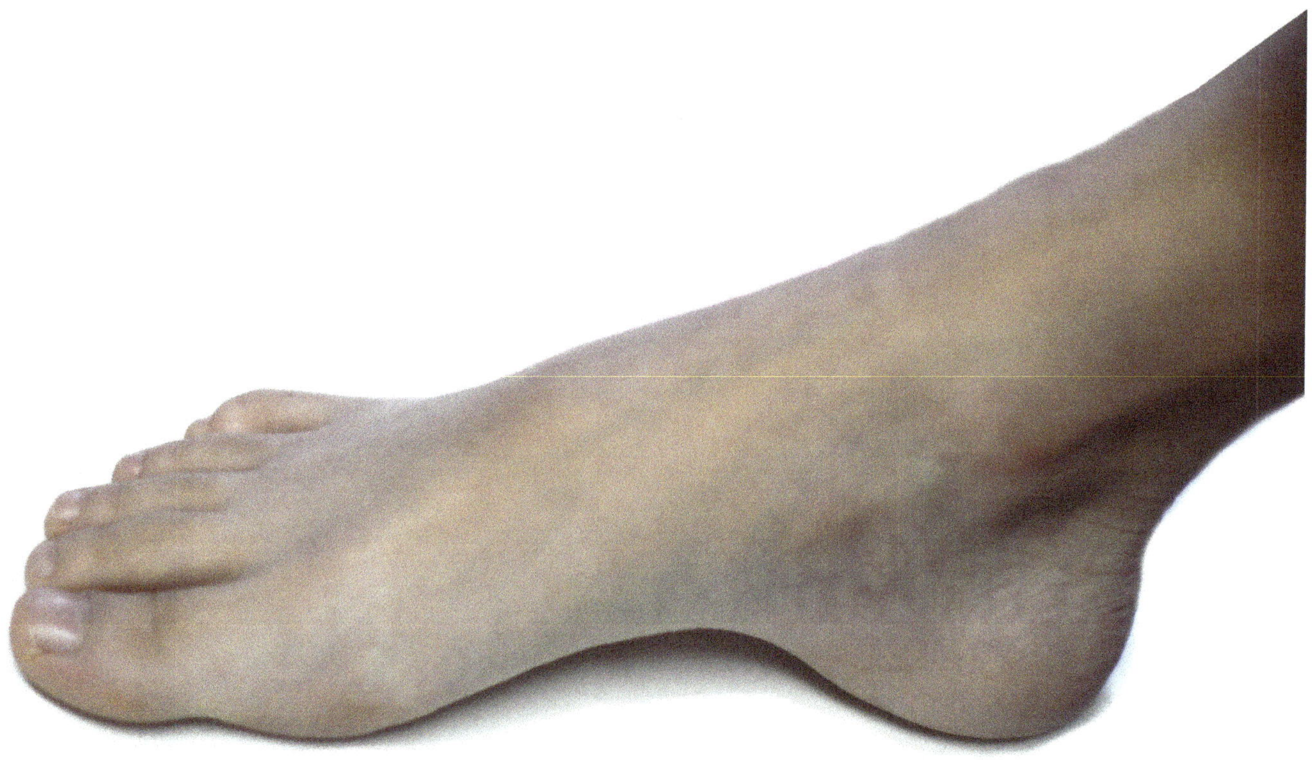

FOOT IN CHARCOAL: PRACTICE II

Now try drawing the foot yourself without the grid.

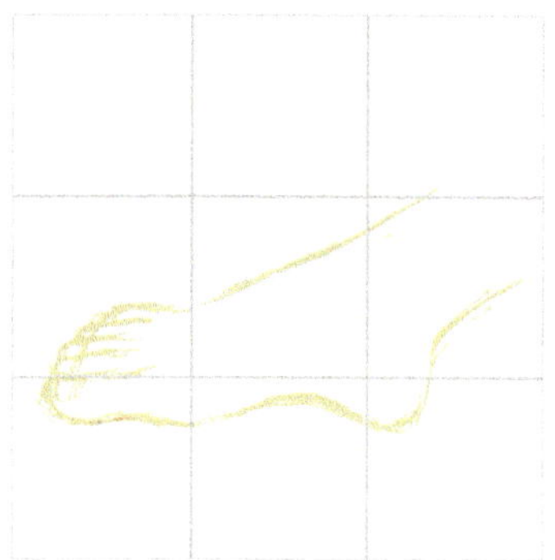

First sketch the general features of the foot area using a light yellow pastel color.

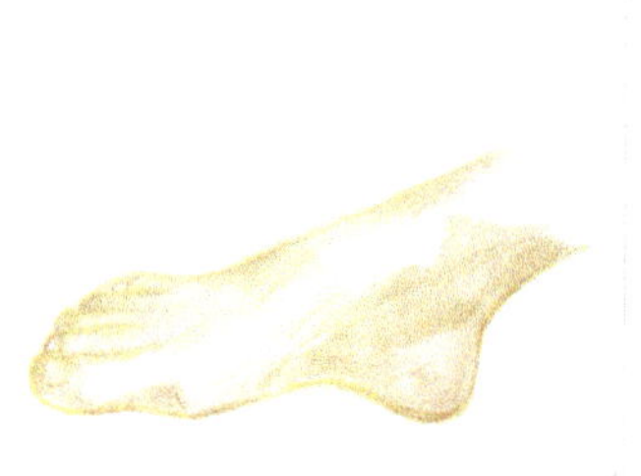

Block in the general areas of shadow and light using a light orange and yellow ochre.

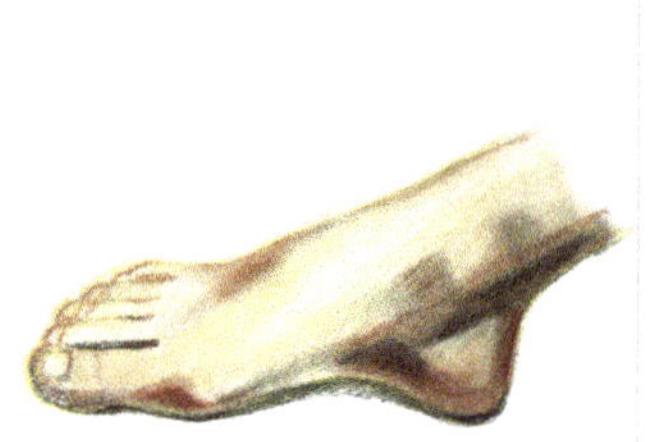

Identify the areas of light, shadow, and reflection light by layering on different light yellows, orange, light green, and pink to create rich skin tones.

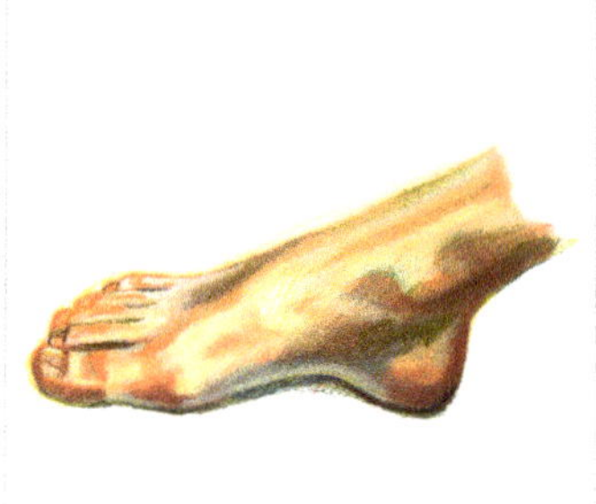

Continue to render the volume of the foot, paying attention to the subtleties in light,shadow and reflection lights. Continue to blend and add more pinks, greens and browns to create rich colors.

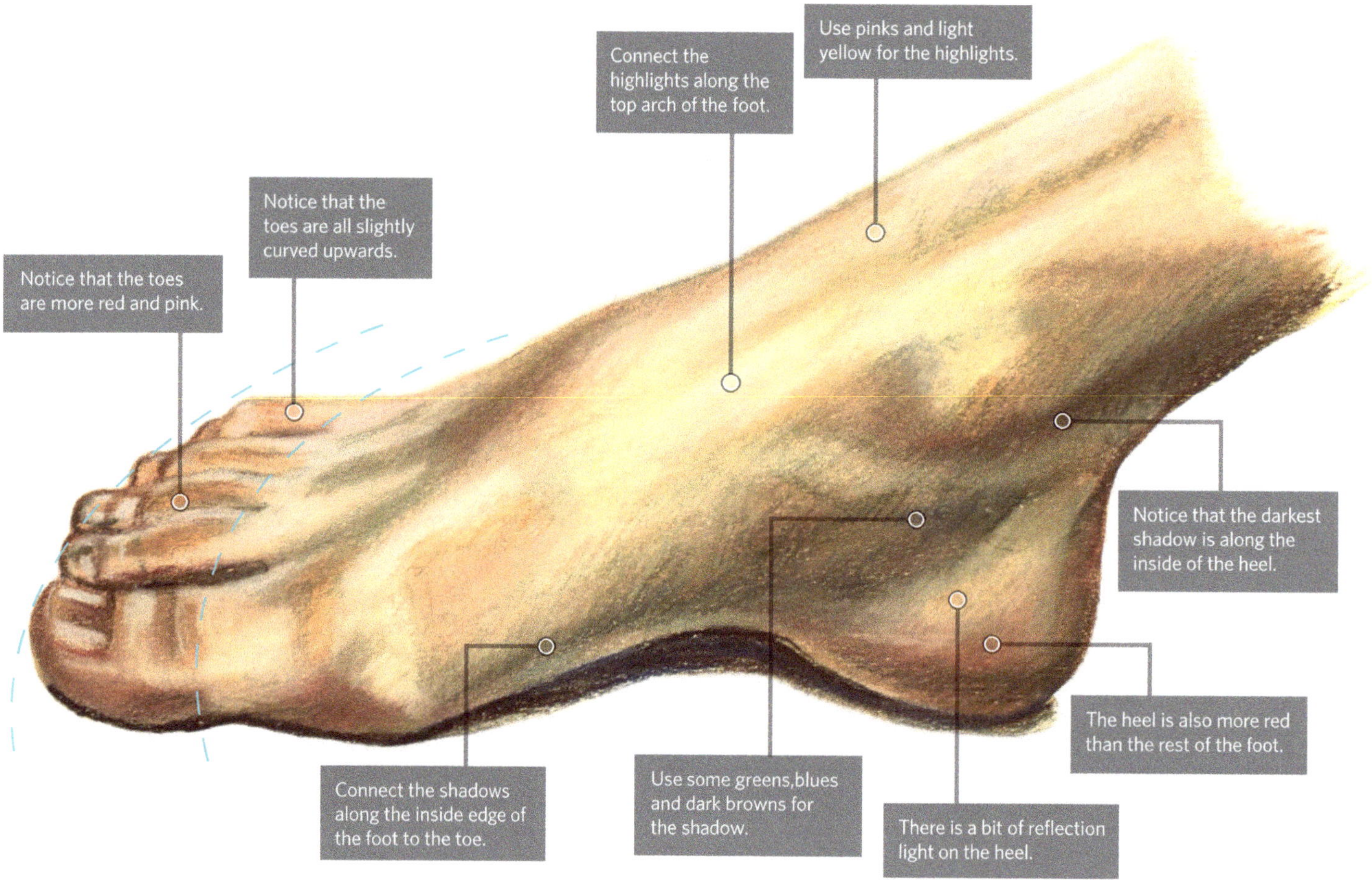

Connect the highlights along the top arch of the foot.

Use pinks and light yellow for the highlights.

Notice that the toes are all slightly curved upwards.

Notice that the toes are more red and pink.

Notice that the darkest shadow is along the inside of the heel.

The heel is also more red than the rest of the foot.

Connect the shadows along the inside edge of the foot to the toe.

Use some greens,blues and dark browns for the shadow.

There is a bit of reflection light on the heel.

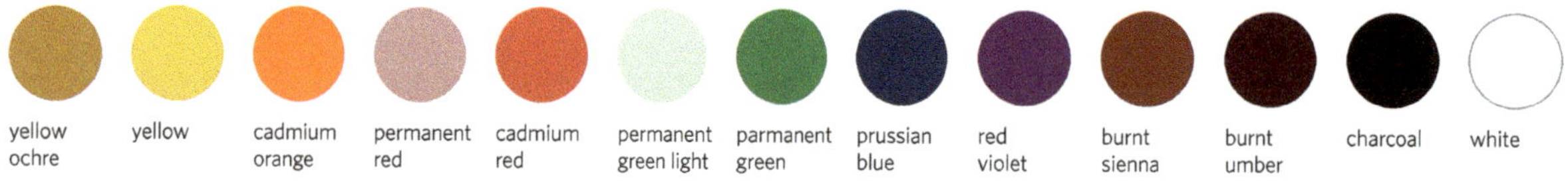

yellow ochre | yellow | cadmium orange | permanent red | cadmium red | permanent green light | parmanent green | prussian blue | red violet | burnt sienna | burnt umber | charcoal | white

Now try drawing the foot yourself.

Now that you have practiced how to draw a right foot in pastel following a step-by-step tutorial, use the page on the right to try and draw from life. You can draw from the picture below, use a mirror, or ask a friend to sit for you and try different variations of compositions.

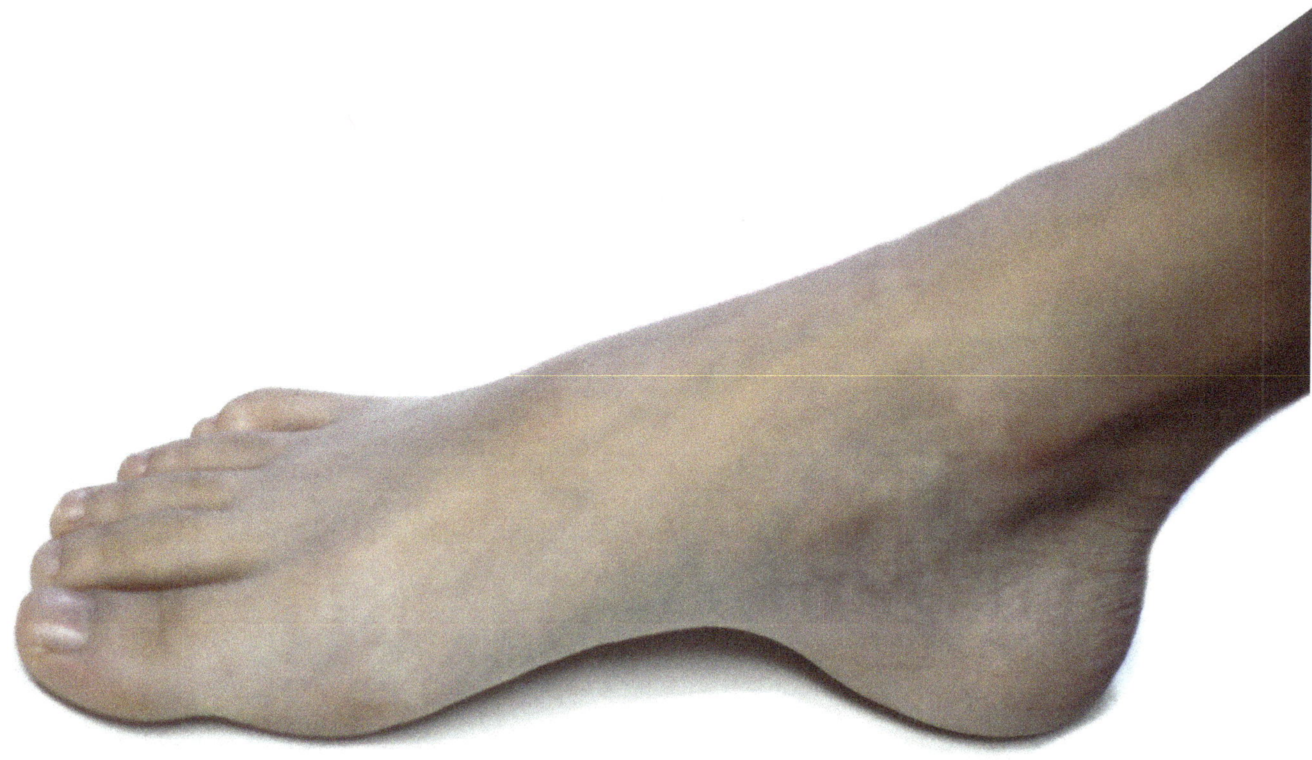

Now try drawing the foot yourself without the grid.

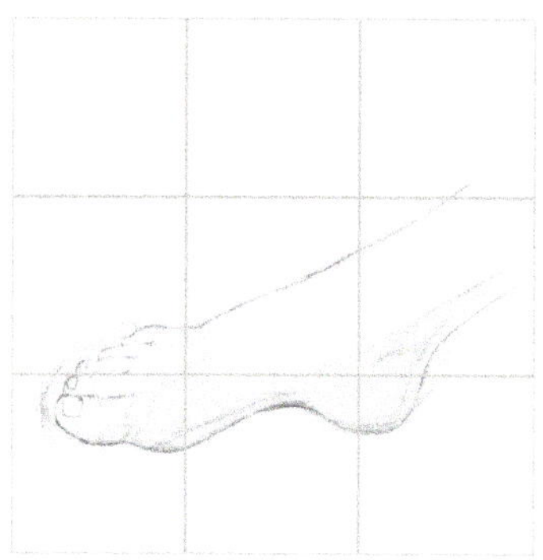

Begin by lightly creating an outline of the foot in pencil.

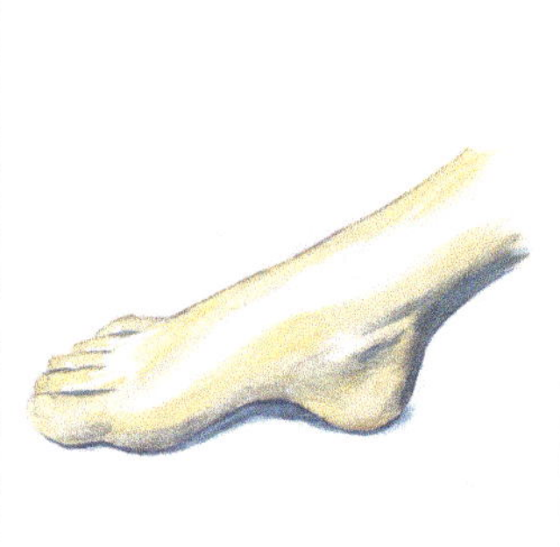

Block in the general areas of color, using yellow and green.

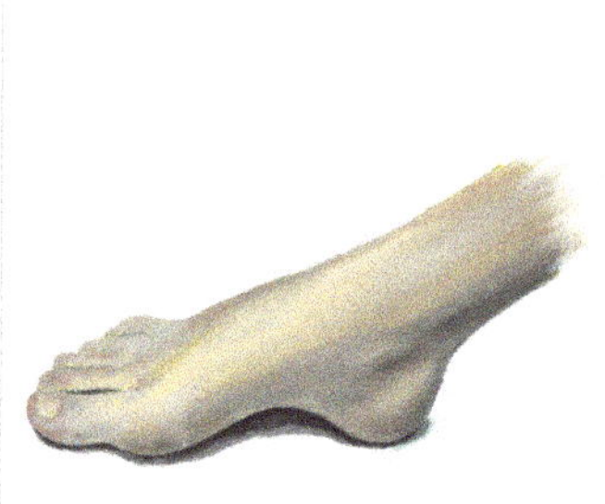

Identify the areas of light, shadow, and reflection light by mixing in different light yellows, orange, light green, and pink to create rich skin tones.

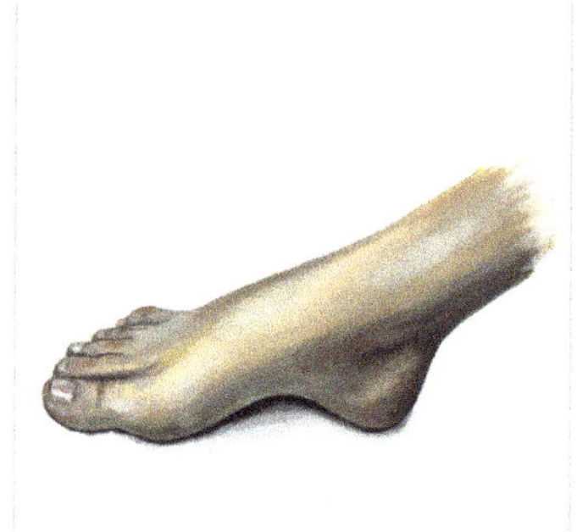

Continue to render the volume of the foot, paying attention to the subtleties in light,shadow and reflection lights. Continue to blend and add more pinks, greens and browns to create rich colors.

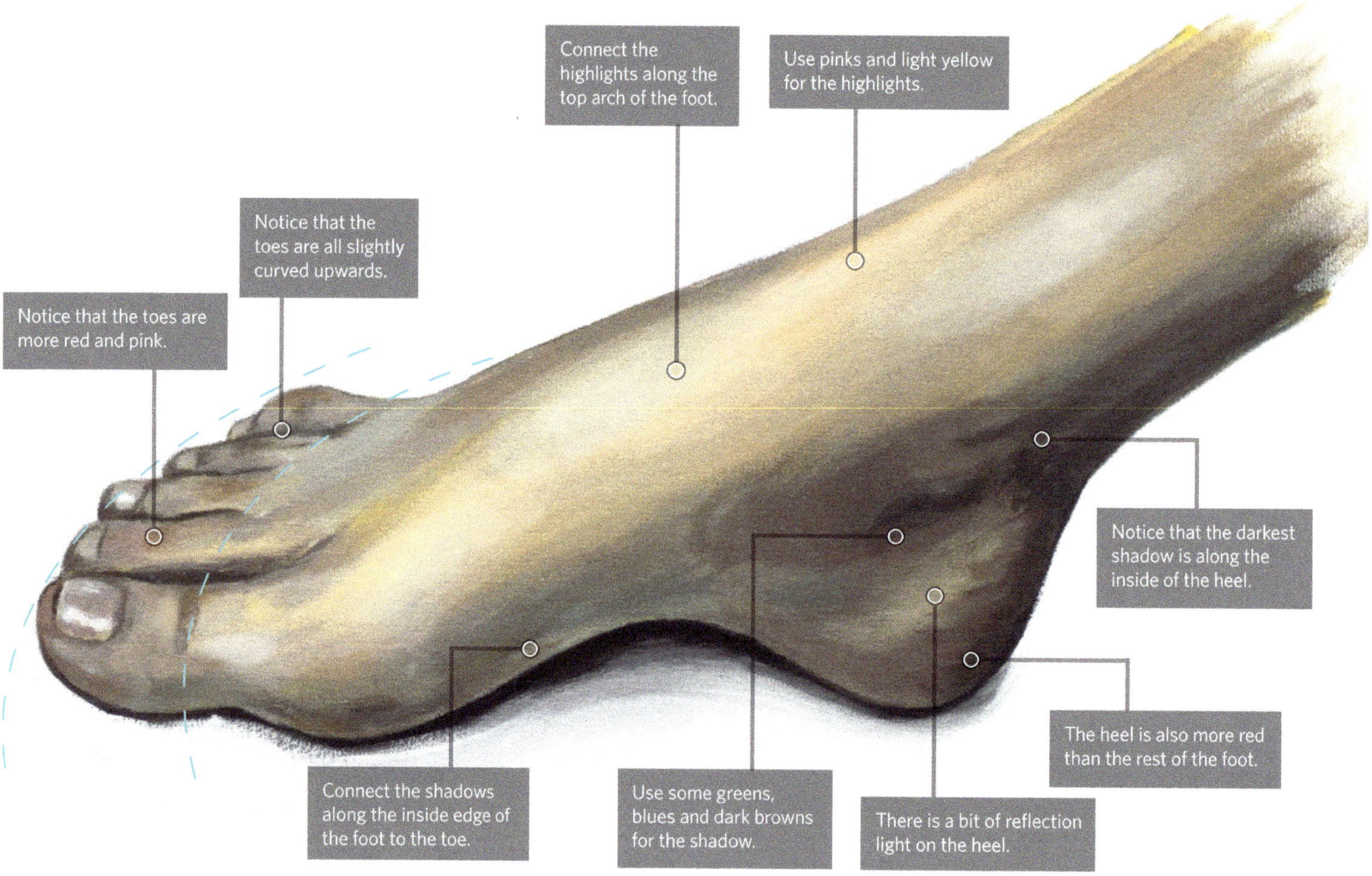

Connect the highlights along the top arch of the foot.

Use pinks and light yellow for the highlights.

Notice that the toes are all slightly curved upwards.

Notice that the toes are more red and pink.

Notice that the darkest shadow is along the inside of the heel.

The heel is also more red than the rest of the foot.

Connect the shadows along the inside edge of the foot to the toe.

Use some greens, blues and dark browns for the shadow.

There is a bit of reflection light on the heel.

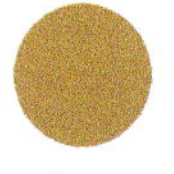

yellow ochre

yellow

cadmium orange

permanent red

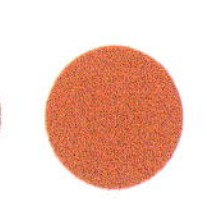

cadmium red

permanent green light

parmanent green

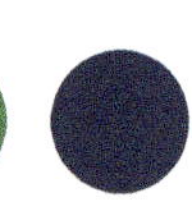

prussian blue

red violet

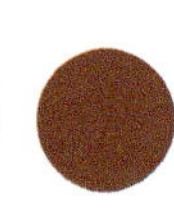

burnt sienna

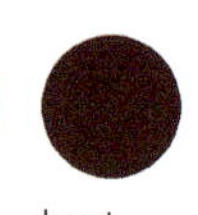

burnt umber

charcoal

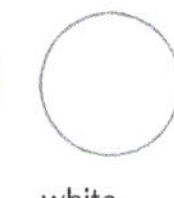

white

Now try painting the foot yourself.

Now that you have practiced how to paint a right foot in acrylic following a step-by-step tutorial, use the page on the right to try and paint from life. You can paint from the picture below, use a mirror, or ask a friend to sit for you and try different variations of compositions.

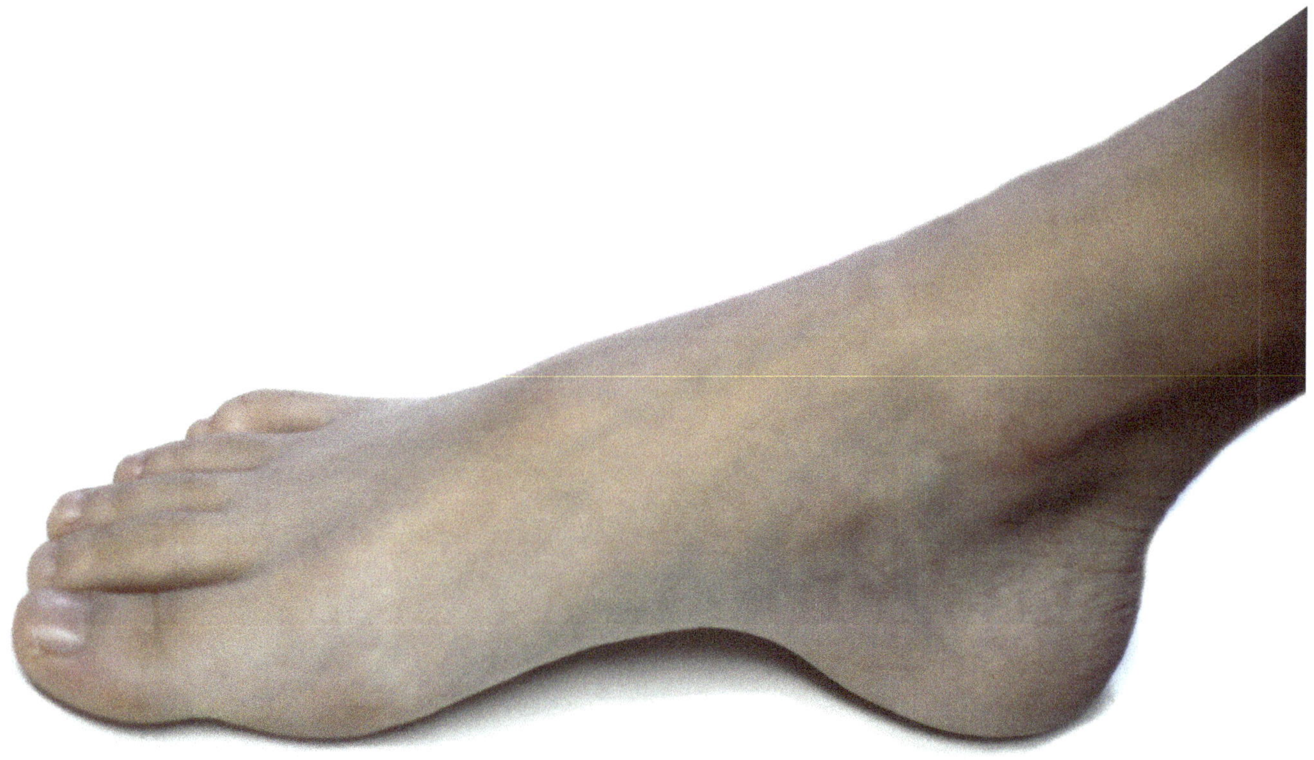

Now try painting the foot yourself without the grid.

Now that you have practiced how to draw and paint feet in charcoal, pastel, and acrylic following step-by-step tutorials, use the page on the right to try and draw from life. You can draw from the picture below, use a mirror, or ask a friend to sit for you and try different variations of perspectives to help better your understanding of the structure of feet.

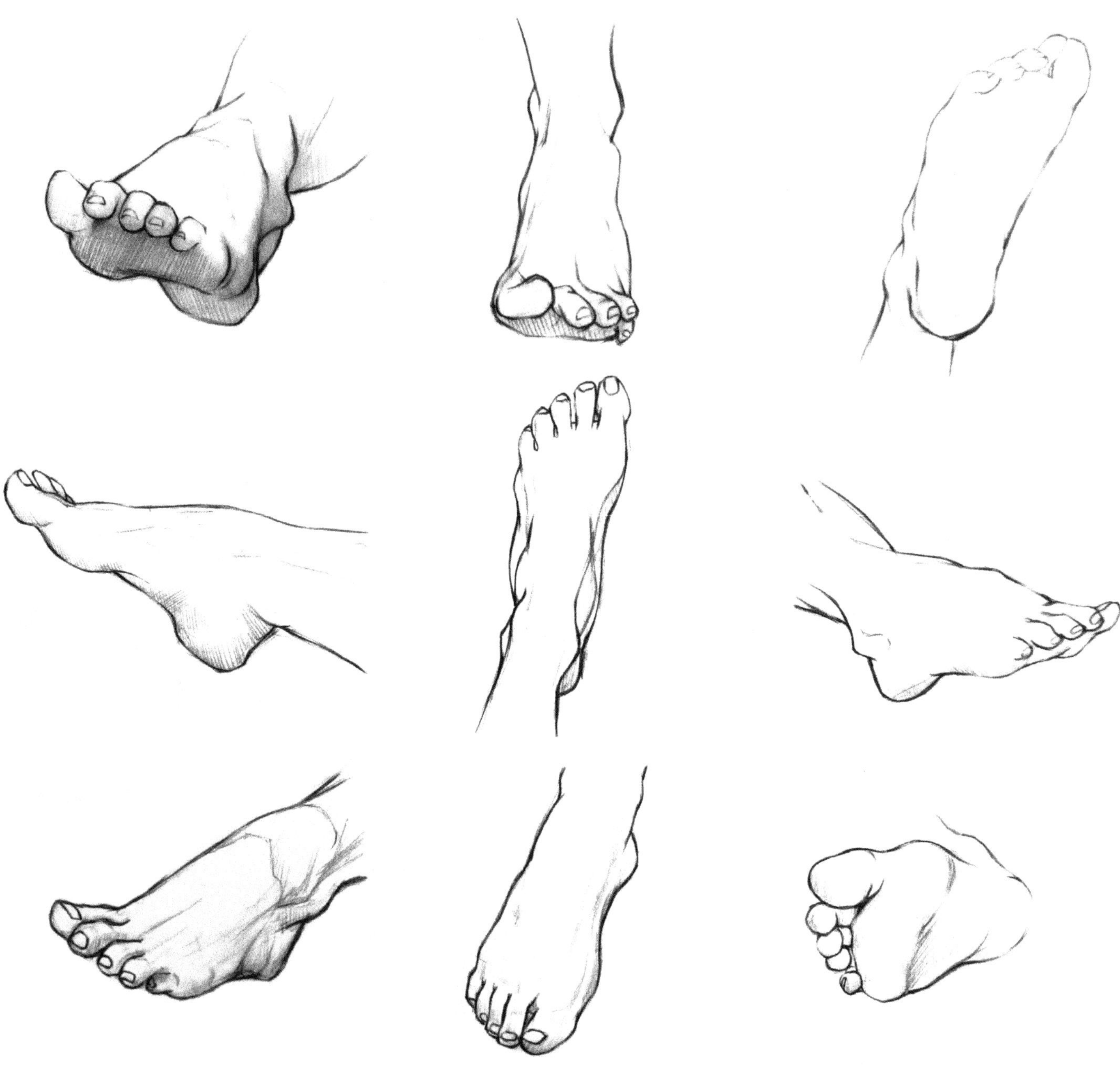

Now try drawing these foot positions yourself.

The knee is a joint that connects the lower and upper leg. Around these bones, in particular, are some of the largest muscles in the body. The angles of the knees help dictate body language, showing whether a person is tense or relaxed, as well as showing which leg they are resting their weight on. There is very little muscle mass around the bones of the knee itself, so this should be one of the thinnest parts of the leg, second to the ankle.

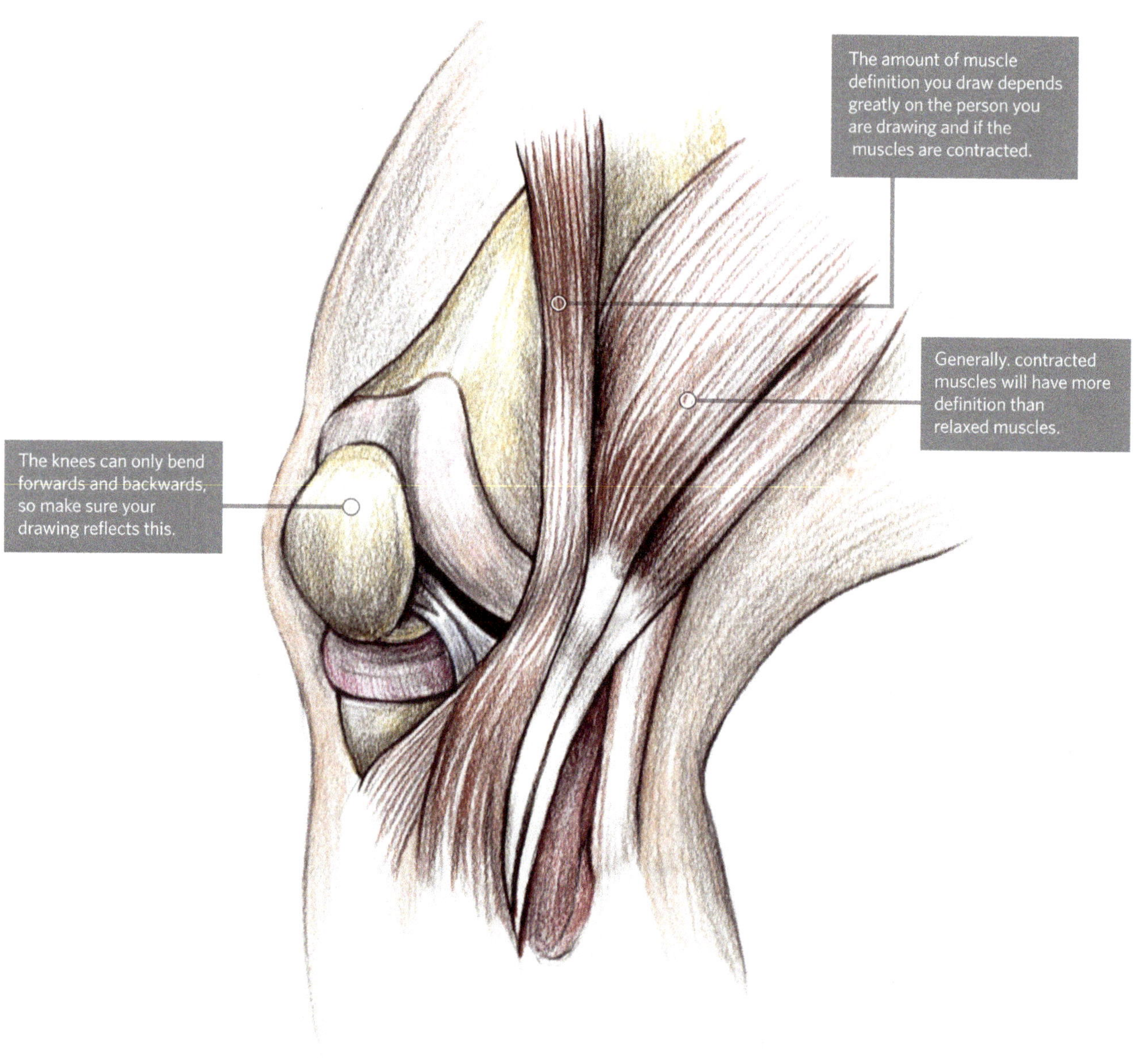

PRACTICE

Now try drawing knee anatomy yourself.

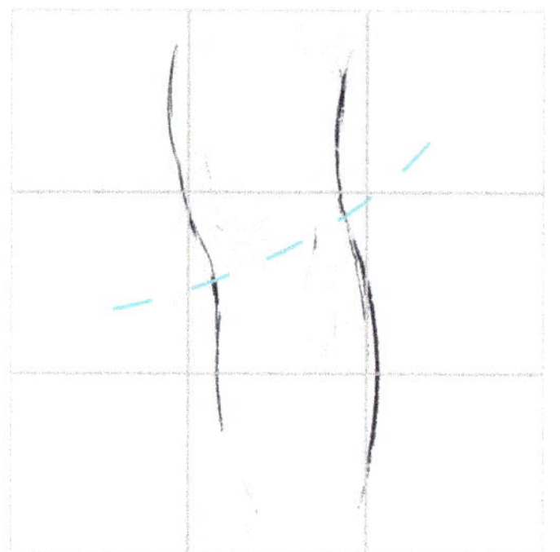
Begin by lightly creating an outline of the knee in vine charcoal.

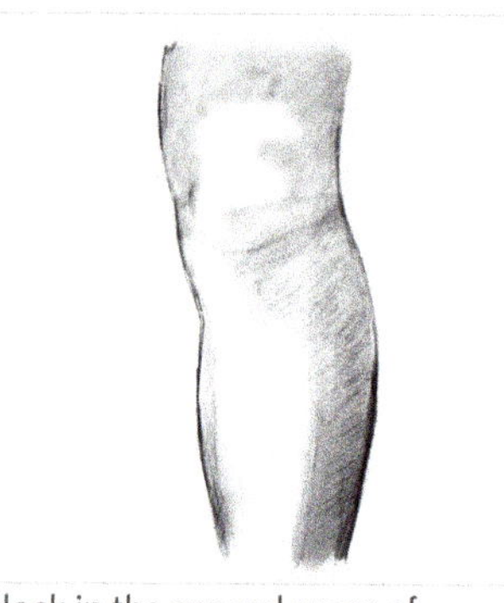
Block in the general areas of shadow and light on the knee.

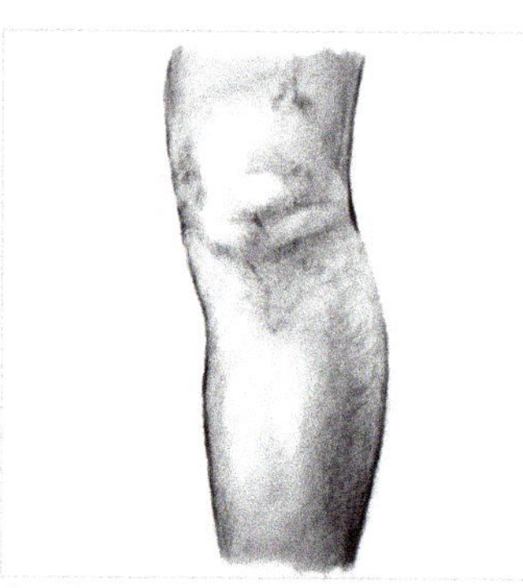
Continue to render the volume of the knee by introducing compressed charcoal.

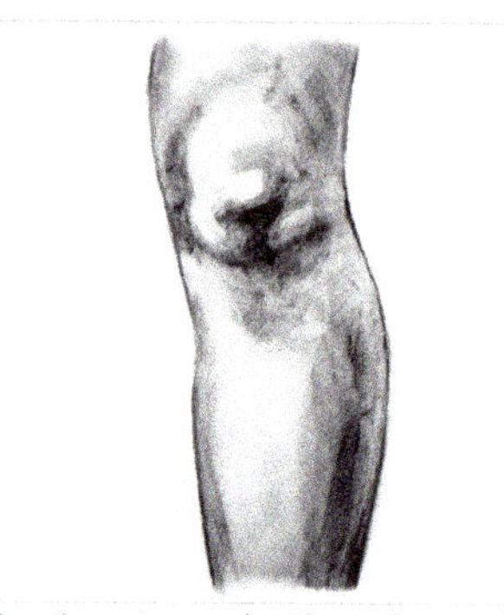
Continue to render the volume of the knee, paying attention to the general geometric shapes of the knee and how light hits the leg.

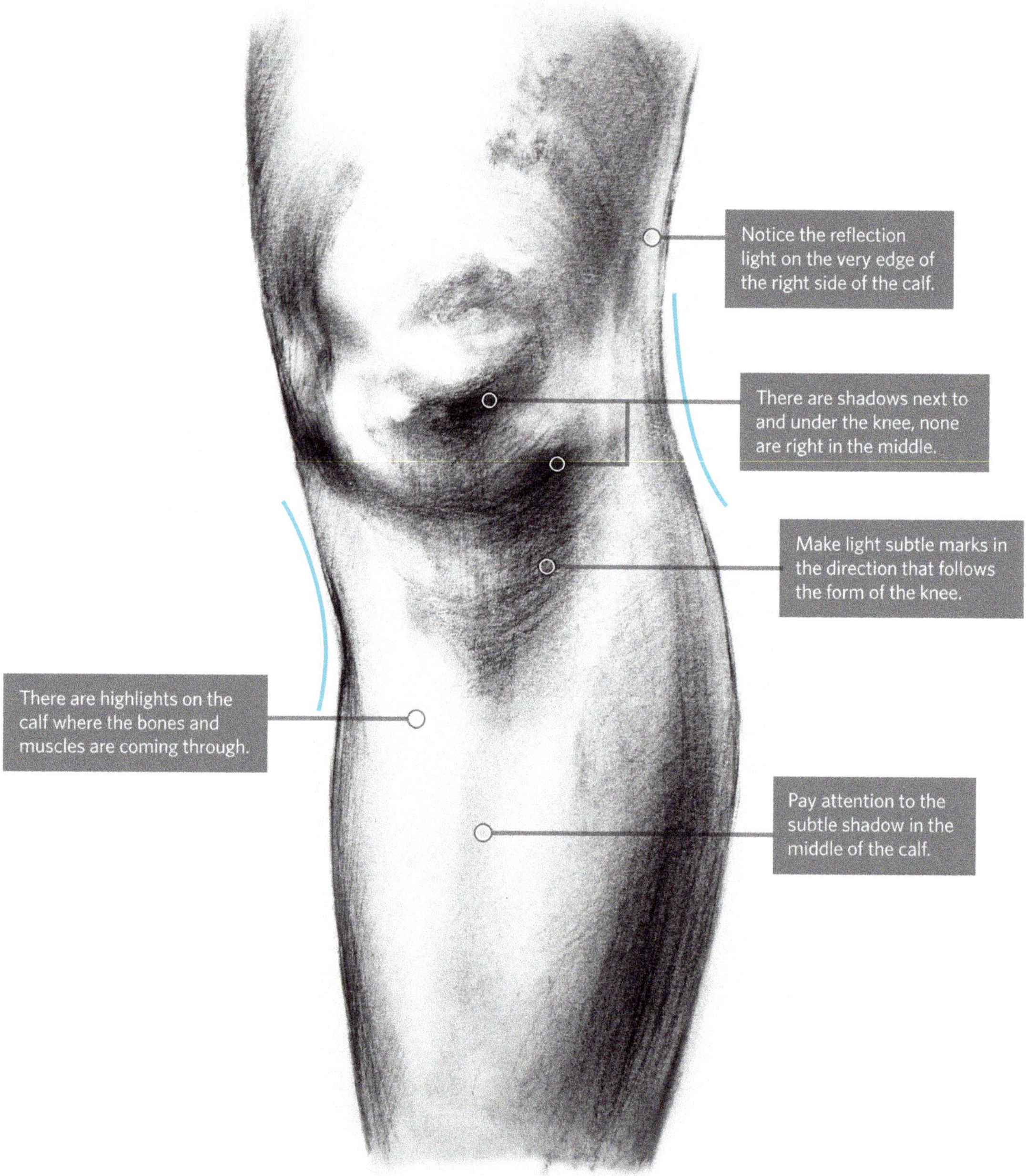

Notice the reflection light on the very edge of the right side of the calf.

There are shadows next to and under the knee, none are right in the middle.

Make light subtle marks in the direction that follows the form of the knee.

There are highlights on the calf where the bones and muscles are coming through.

Pay attention to the subtle shadow in the middle of the calf.

Now try drawing the knee yourself.

Now that you have practiced how to draw an knee in charcoal following a step-by-step tutorial, use the page on the right to try and draw from life. You can draw from the picture below, use a mirror, or ask a friend to sit for you and try different variations of compositions.

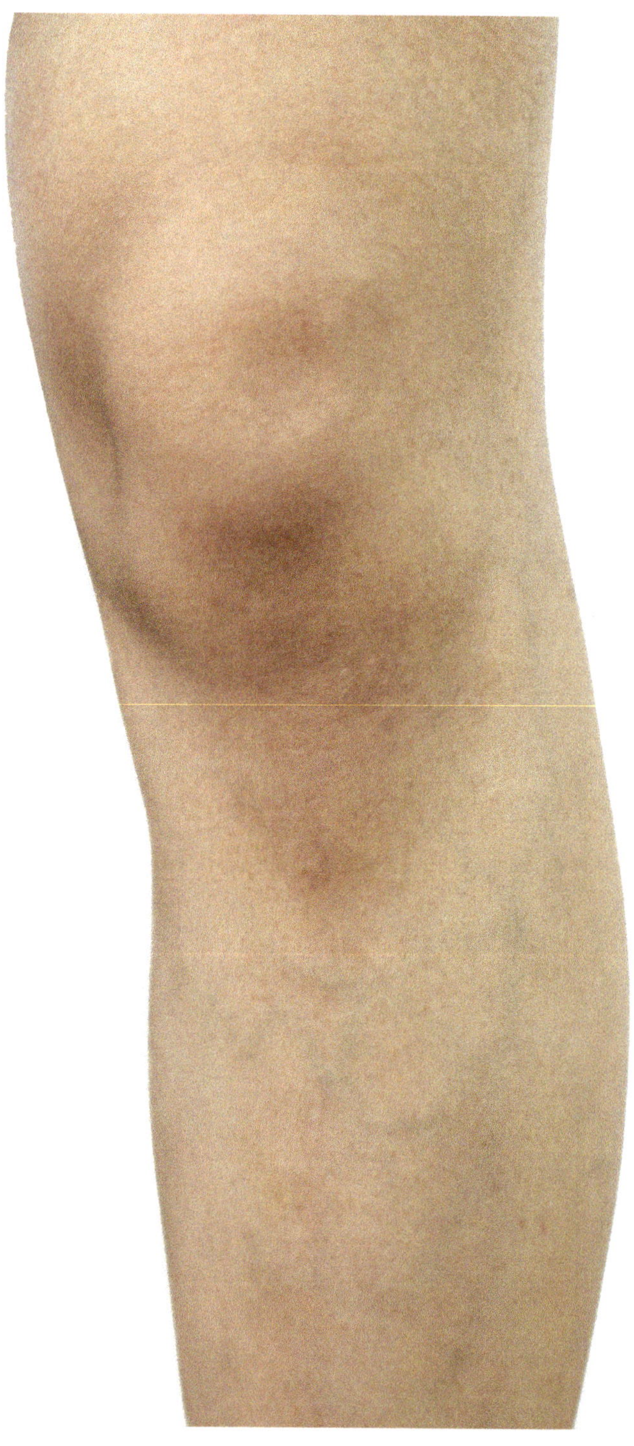

Now try drawing the knee yourself without the grid.

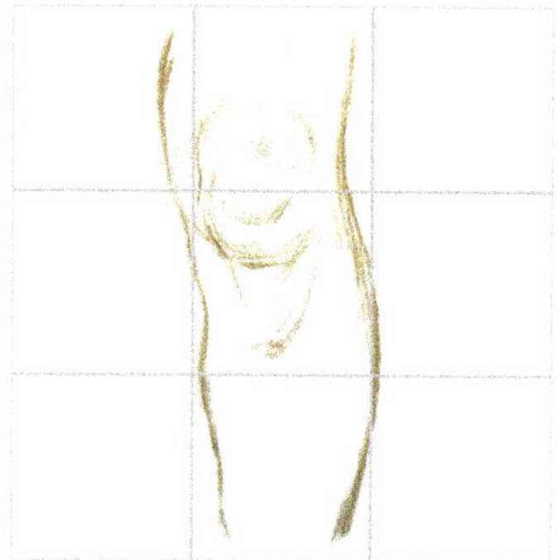
First sketch the general features of the knee area using a light yellow pastel color.

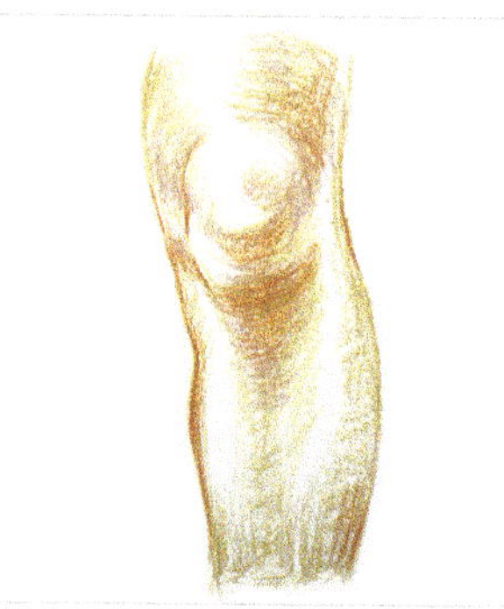
Block in the general areas of shadow and light using a light orange and yellow ochre.

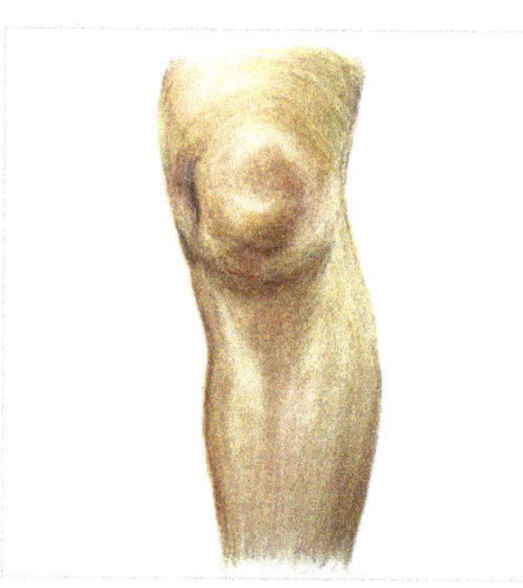
Identify the areas of light, shadow, and reflection light by layering on different light yellows, orange, light green, and pink to create rich skin tones.

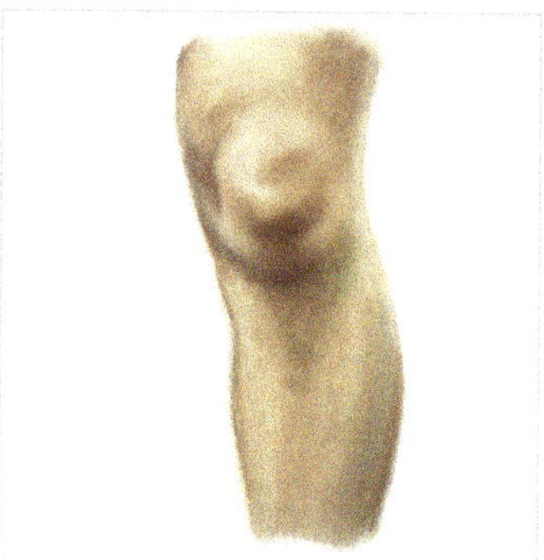
Continue to render the volume of the knee, paying attention to the subtleties in light,shadow and reflection lights. Continue to blend and add more pinks, greens and browns to create rich colors.

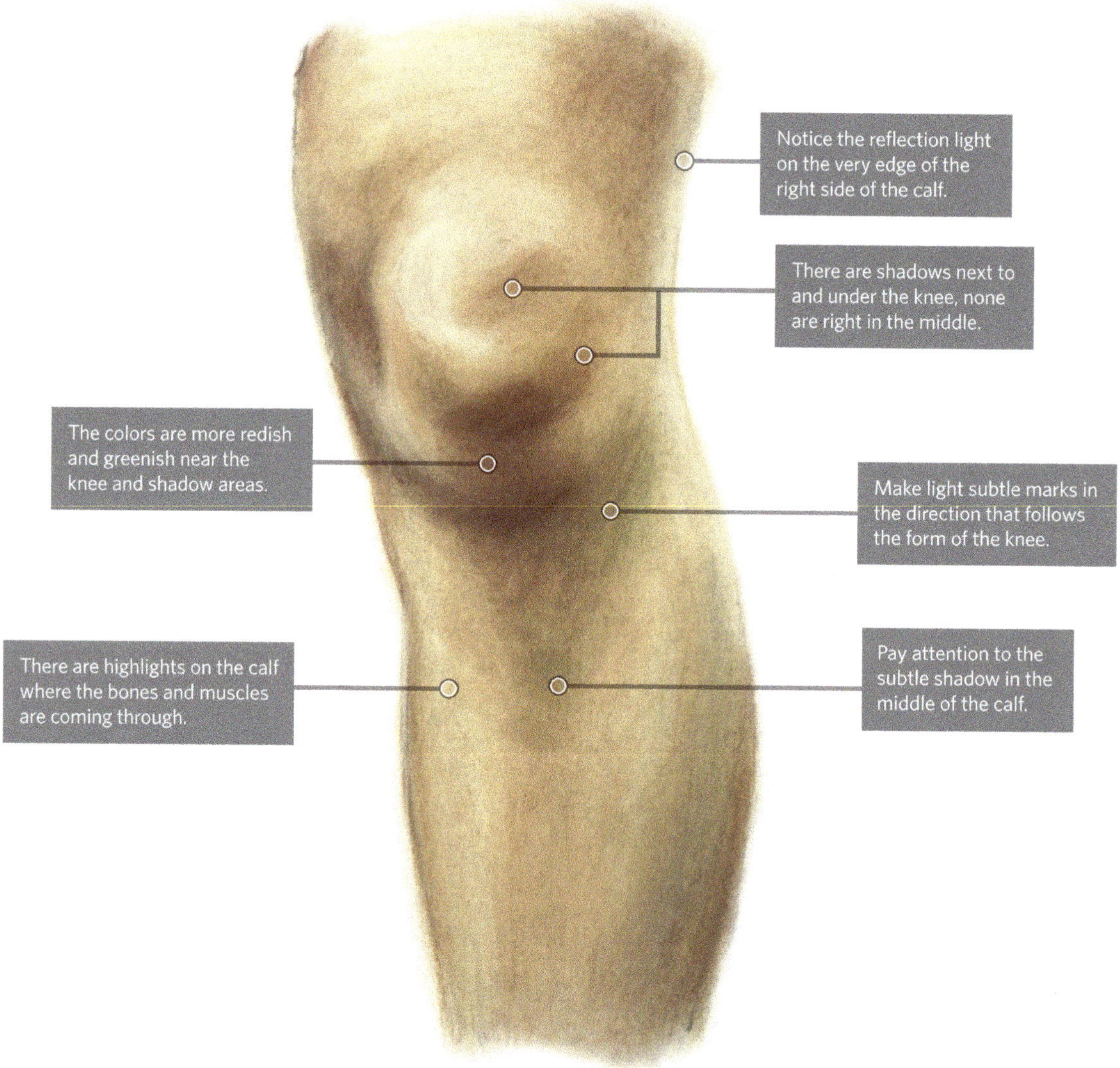

Notice the reflection light on the very edge of the right side of the calf.

There are shadows next to and under the knee, none are right in the middle.

The colors are more redish and greenish near the knee and shadow areas.

Make light subtle marks in the direction that follows the form of the knee.

There are highlights on the calf where the bones and muscles are coming through.

Pay attention to the subtle shadow in the middle of the calf.

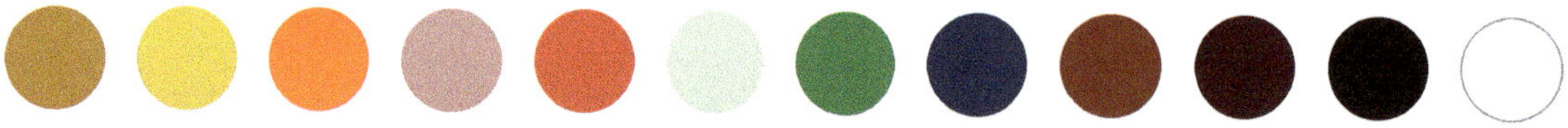

yellow ochre | yellow | cadmium orange | permanent red | cadmium red | permanent green light | parmanent green | prussian blue | burnt sienna | burnt umber | charcoal | white

Now try drawing the knee yourself.

Now that you have practiced how to draw a knee in pastel following a step-by-step tutorial, use the page on the right to try and draw from life. You can draw from the picture below, use a mirror, or ask a friend to sit for you and try different variations of compositions.

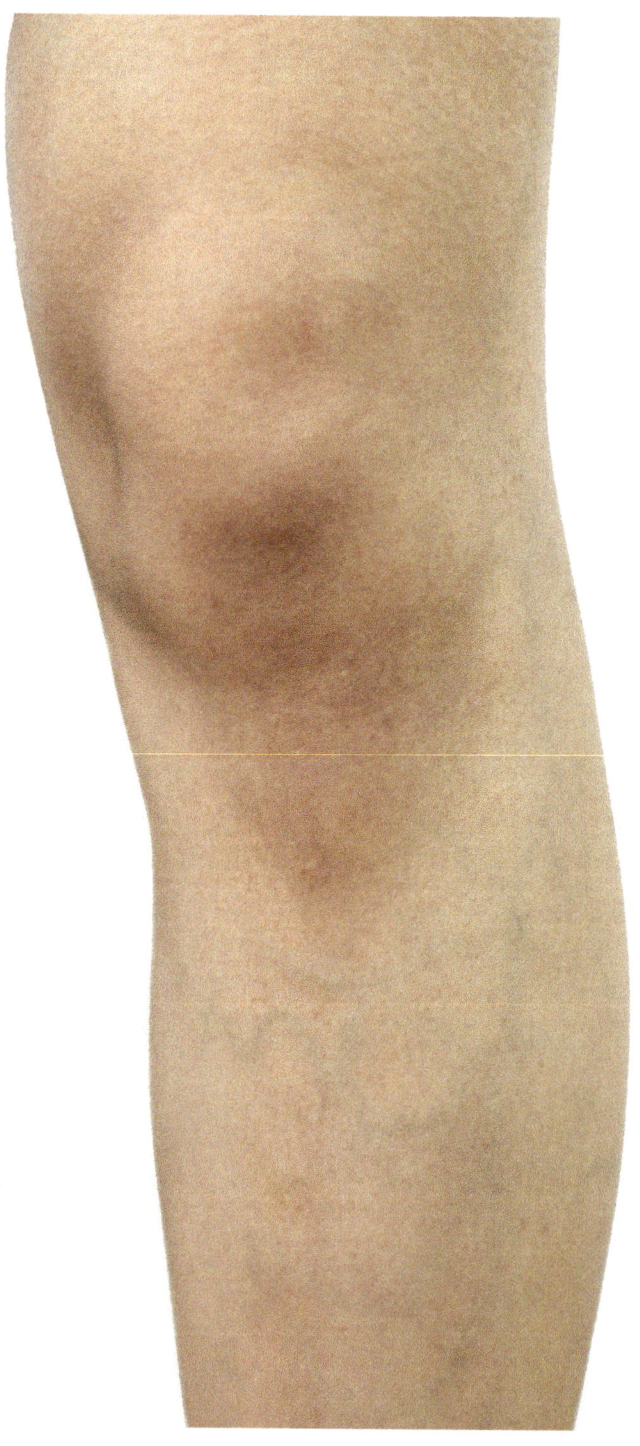

Now try drawing the knee yourself without the grid.

Now that you have practiced different ways the knee can express emotion and how light and shadow affect the knees, try a couple of other perspectives. Pay attention to the shape of the knee in different perspectives.

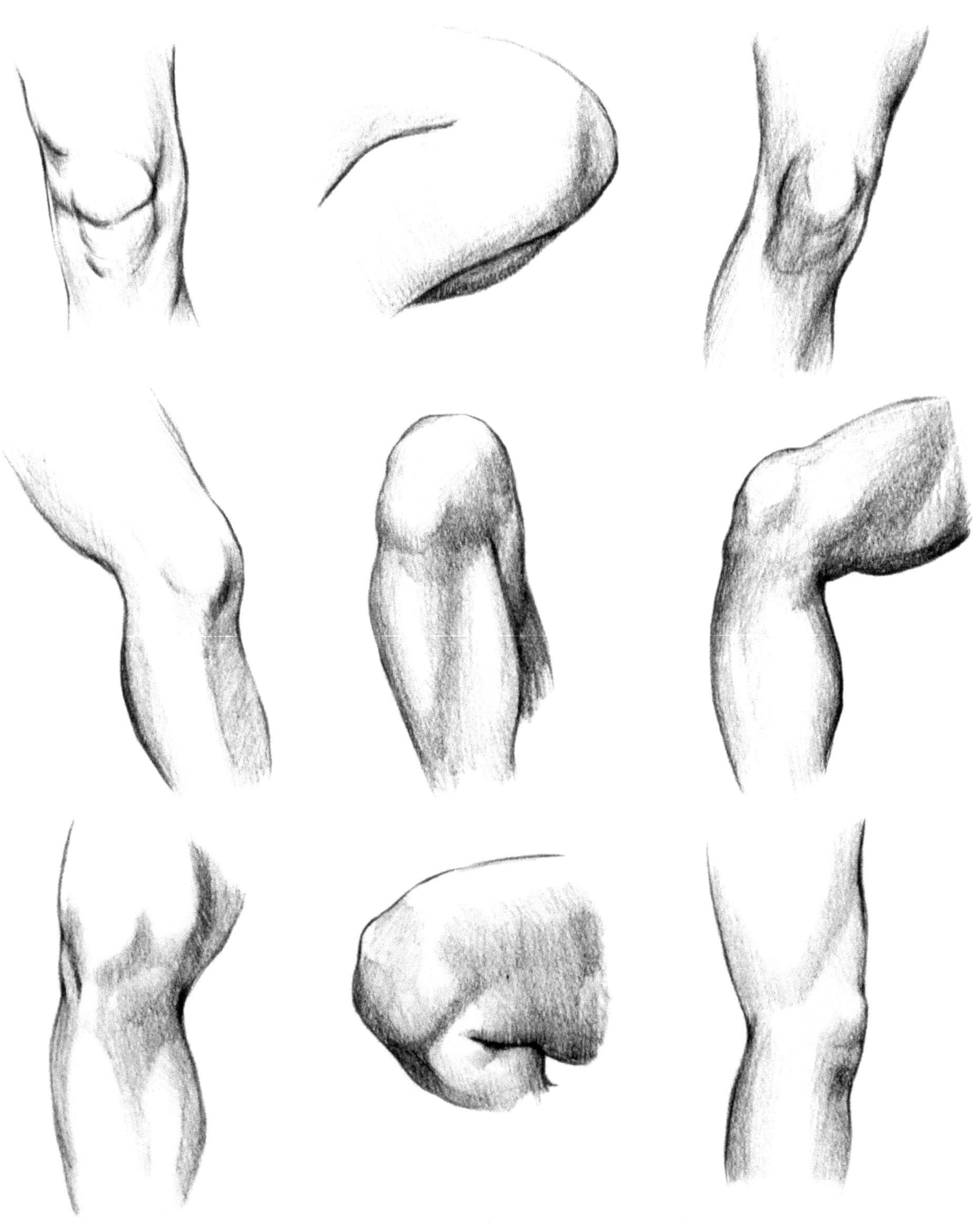

Now try drawing these general knee positions yourself.

The elbow is not only the joint that connects the two bones of the forearm and the upper arm, but where the many muscles of the forearm and the upper arm connect. Therefore the arms need to have more curves than simply two cylinders at an angle. These curves also change depending on which muscles are contracted, which is dictated by the angle of the elbow. For example, if the elbow makes an angle smaller than 90 degrees, the biceps will be contracted, creating a larger curve in the upper arm. Take note that there is very little muscle mass on the bones of the elbow itself, so the skin here should show the shape of the bones lying underneath.

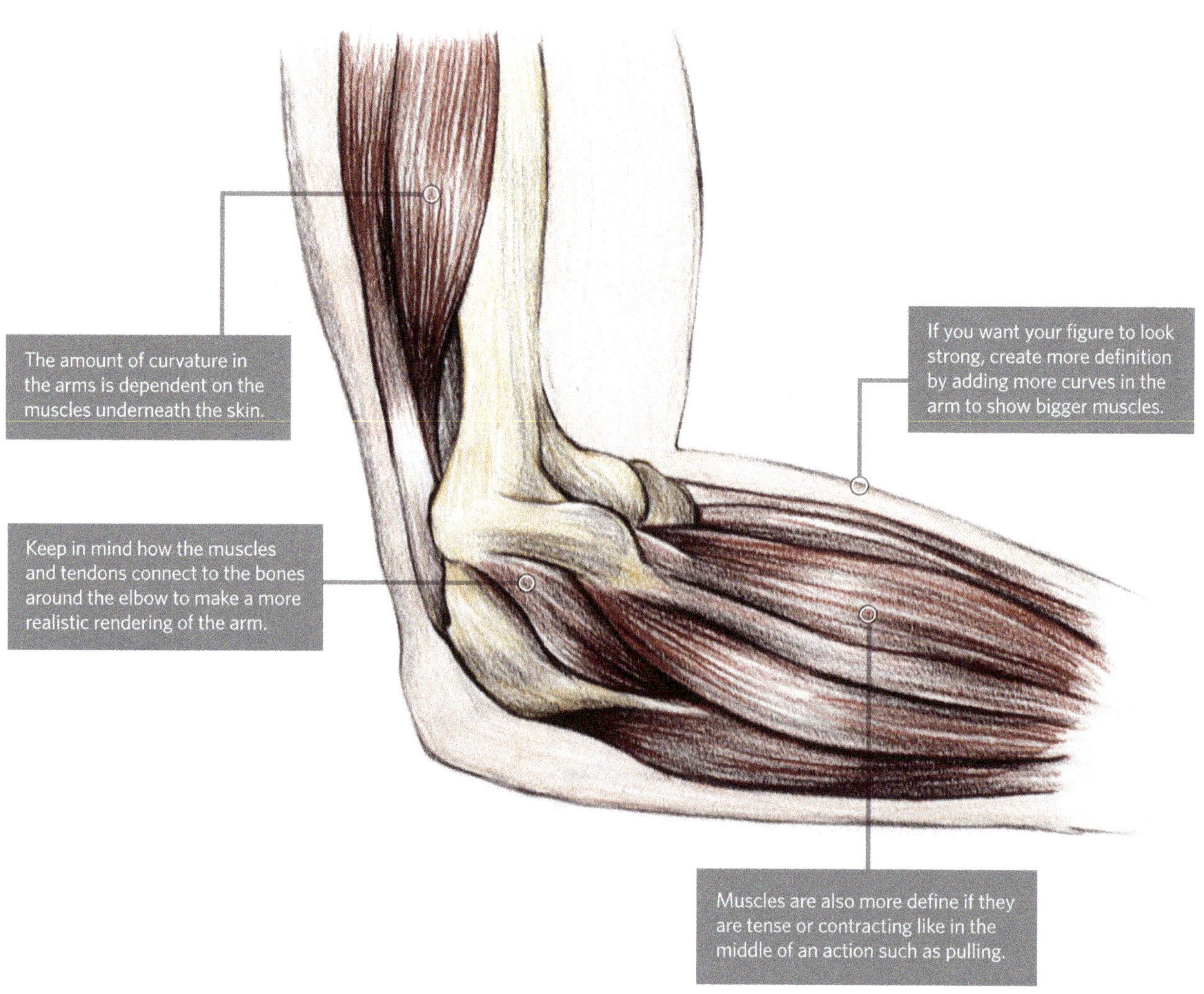

Now try drawing the elbow structure yourself.

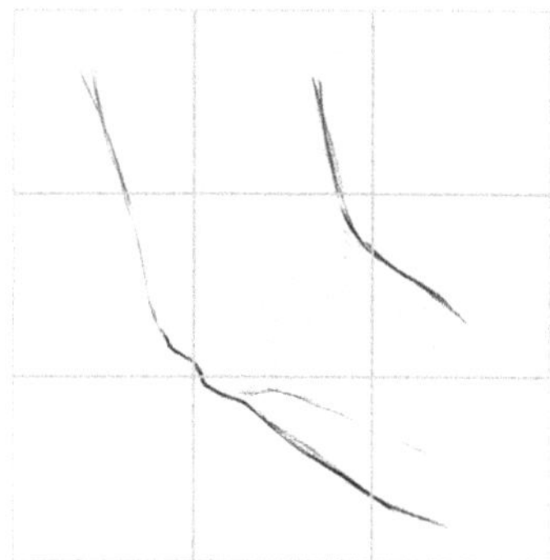
Begin by lightly creating an outline of the elbow in vine charcoal.

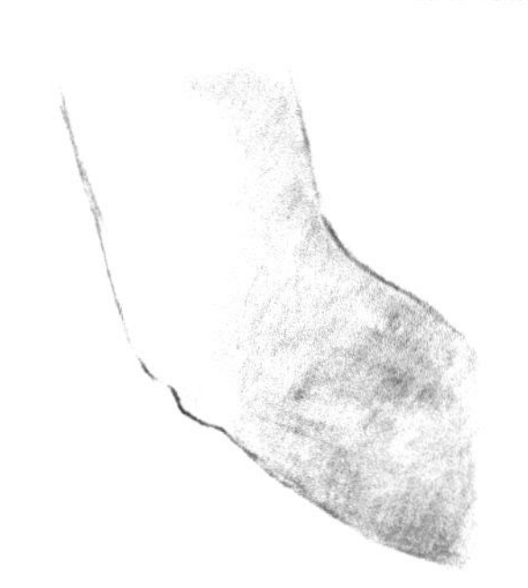
Block in the general areas of shadow and light on the elbow.

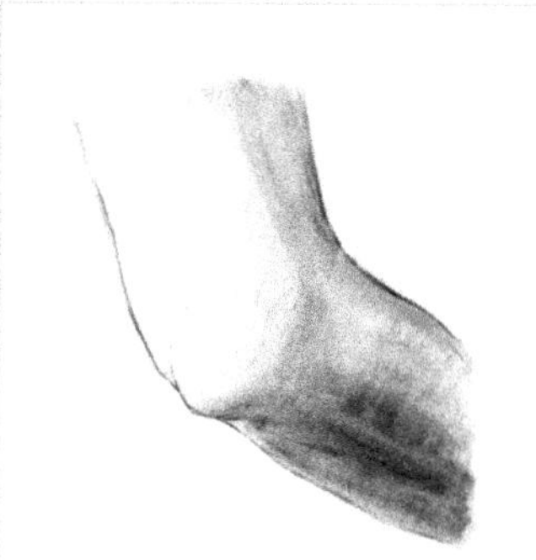
Continue to render the volume of the elbow by introducing compressed charcoal.

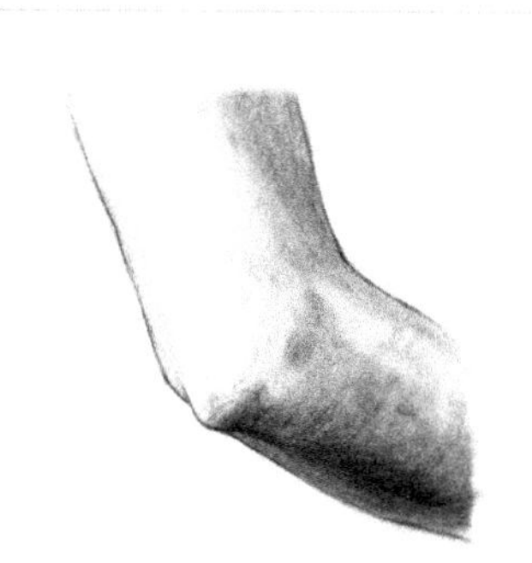
Continue to render the volume of the elbow, paying attention to how to the general geometric shapes of the knee and how light hits the elbow.

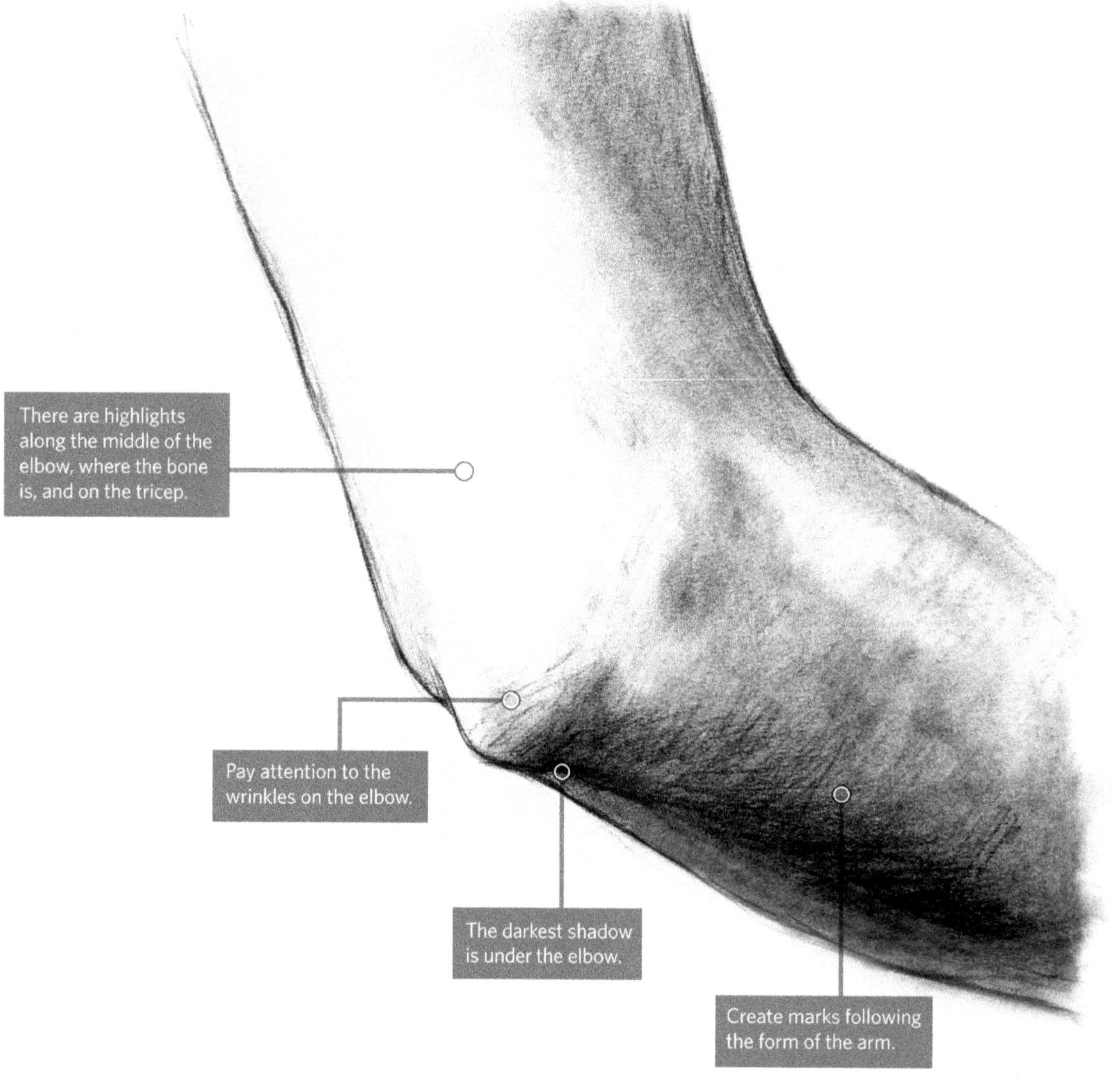

ELBOW IN CHARCOAL: PRACTICE I

Now try drawing the elbow yourself.

Now that you have practiced how to draw an elbow in charcoal following a step-by-step tutorial, use the page on the right to try and draw from life. You can draw from the picture below, use a mirror, or ask a friend to sit for you and try different variations of compositions.

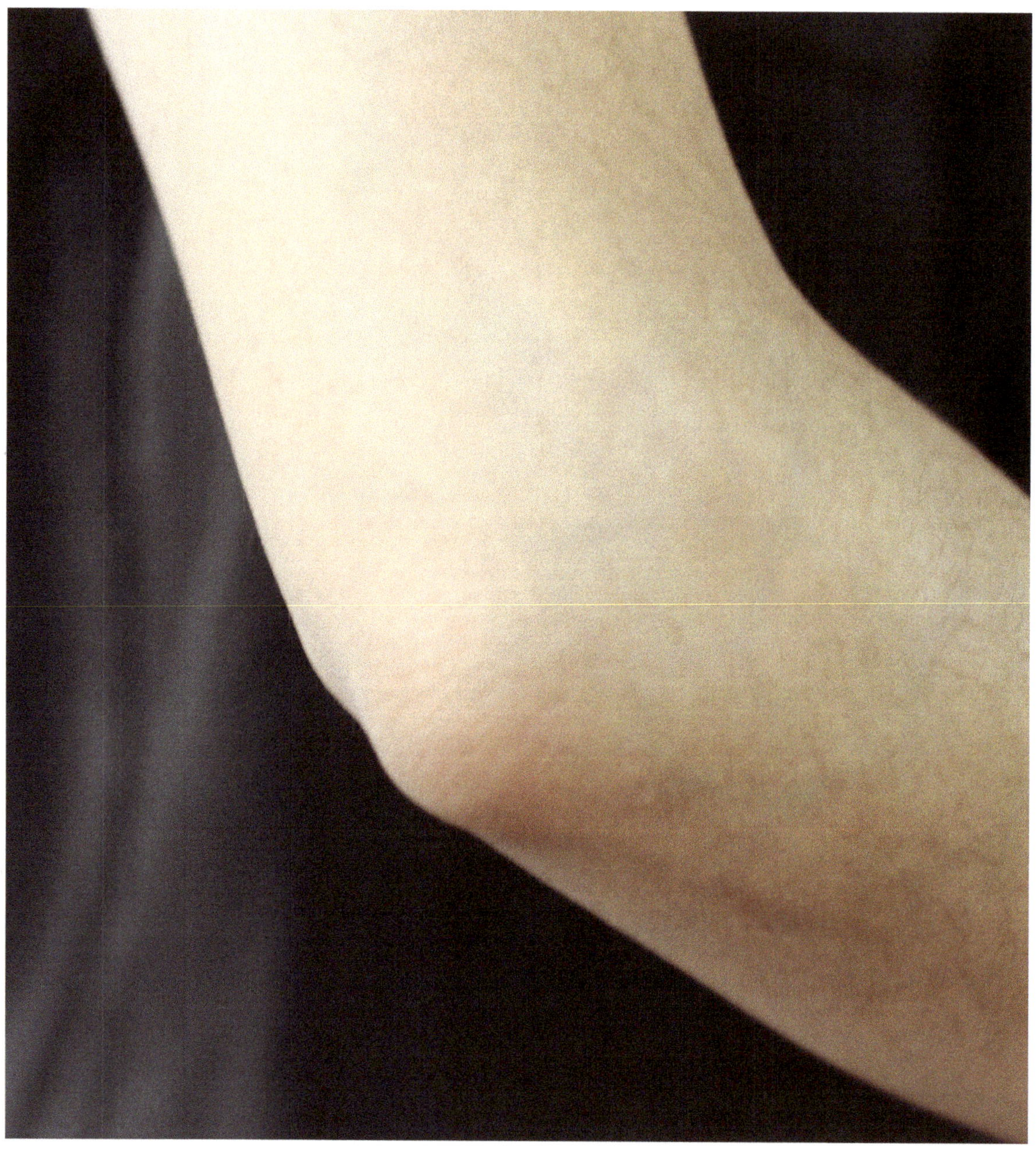

Now try drawing the elbow yourself without the grid.

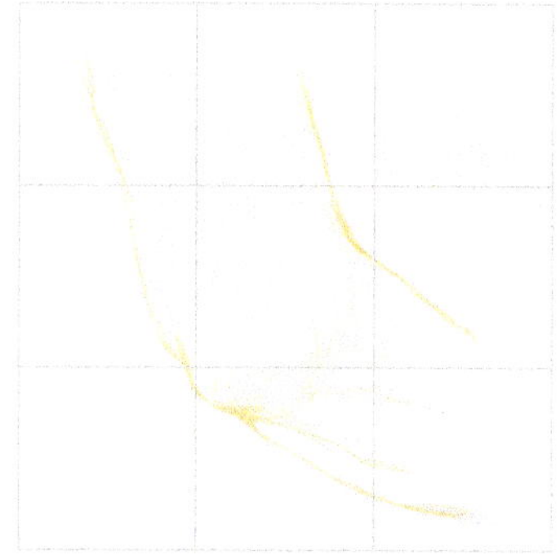

First sketch the general features of the elbow area using a light yellow pastel color.

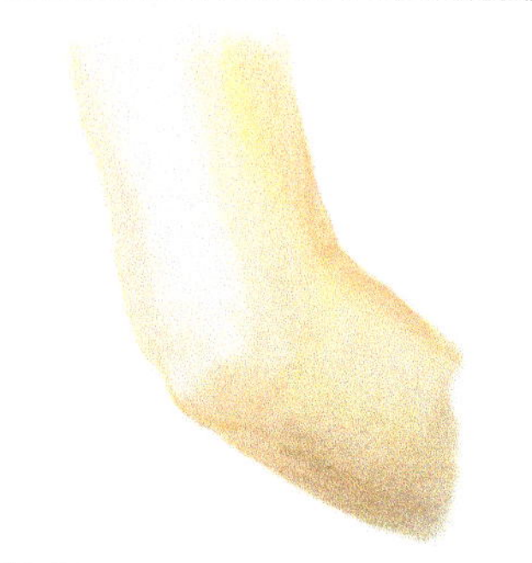

Block in the general areas of shadow and light using a light orange and yellow ochre.

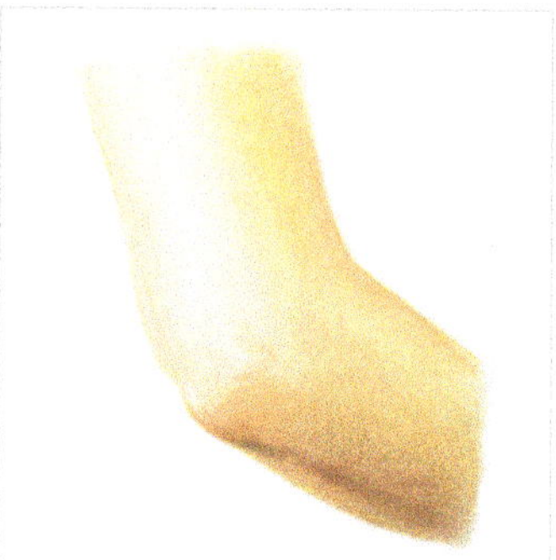

Identify the areas of light, shadow, and reflection light by layering on different light yellows, orange, light green, and pink to create rich skin tones.

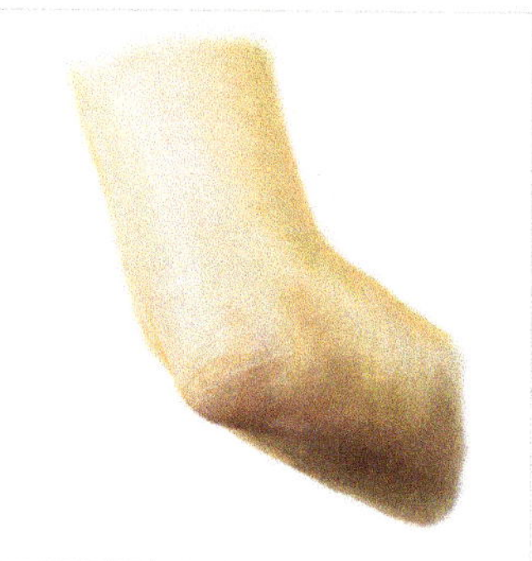

Continue to render the volume of the elbow, paying attention to the subtleties in light,shadow and reflection lights. Continue to blend and add more pinks, greens and browns to create rich colors.

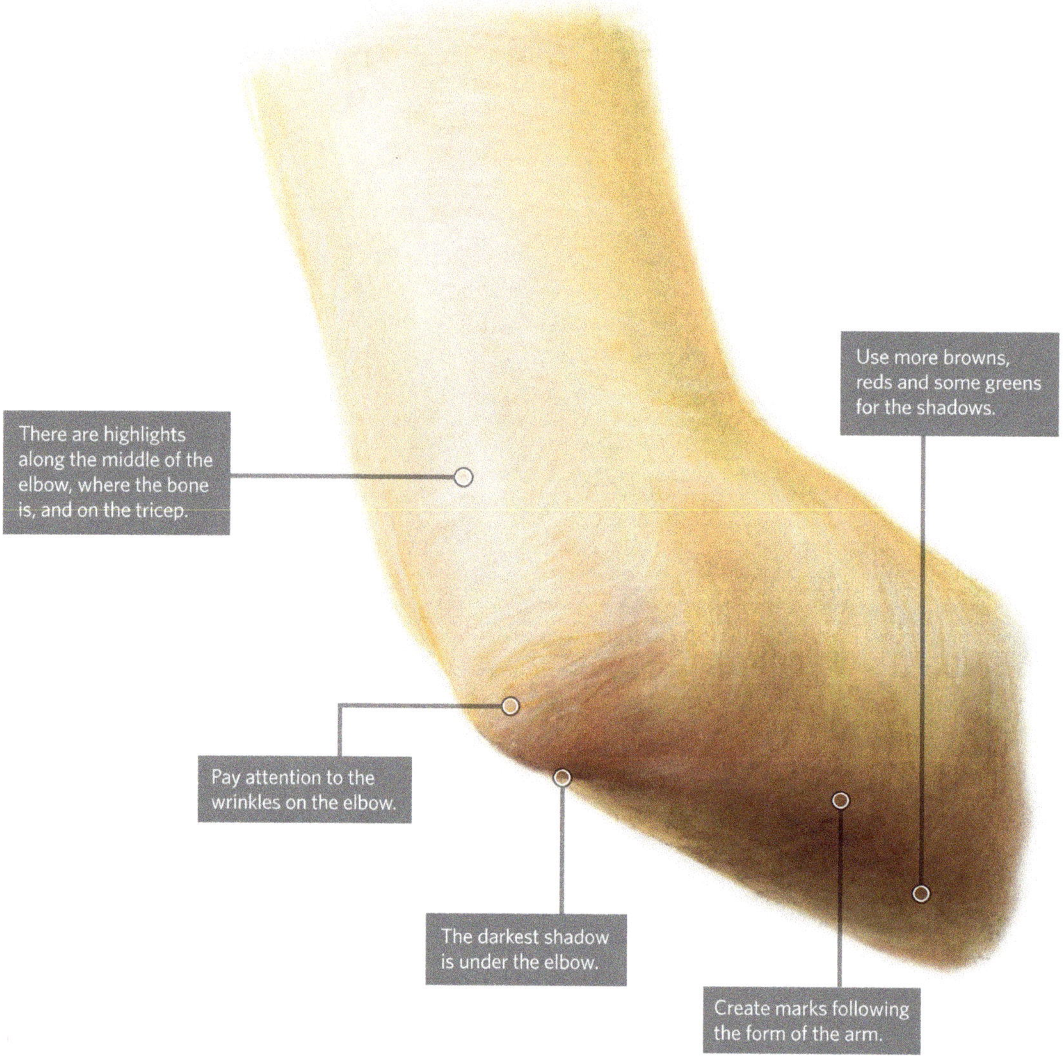

Use more browns, reds and some greens for the shadows.

There are highlights along the middle of the elbow, where the bone is, and on the tricep.

Pay attention to the wrinkles on the elbow.

The darkest shadow is under the elbow.

Create marks following the form of the arm.

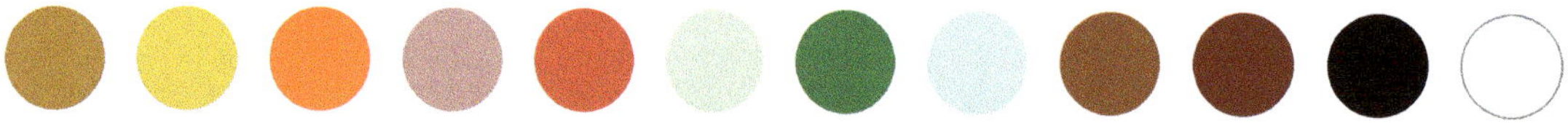

yellow ochre
yellow
cadmium orange
permanent red
cadmium red
permanent green light
parmanent green
light blue
raw sienna
burnt sienna
charcoal
white

Now try drawing the elbow yourself.

Now that you have practiced how to draw an elbow in pastel following a step-by-step tutorial, use the page on the right to try and draw from life. You can draw from the picture below, use a mirror, or ask a friend to sit for you and try different variations of compositions.

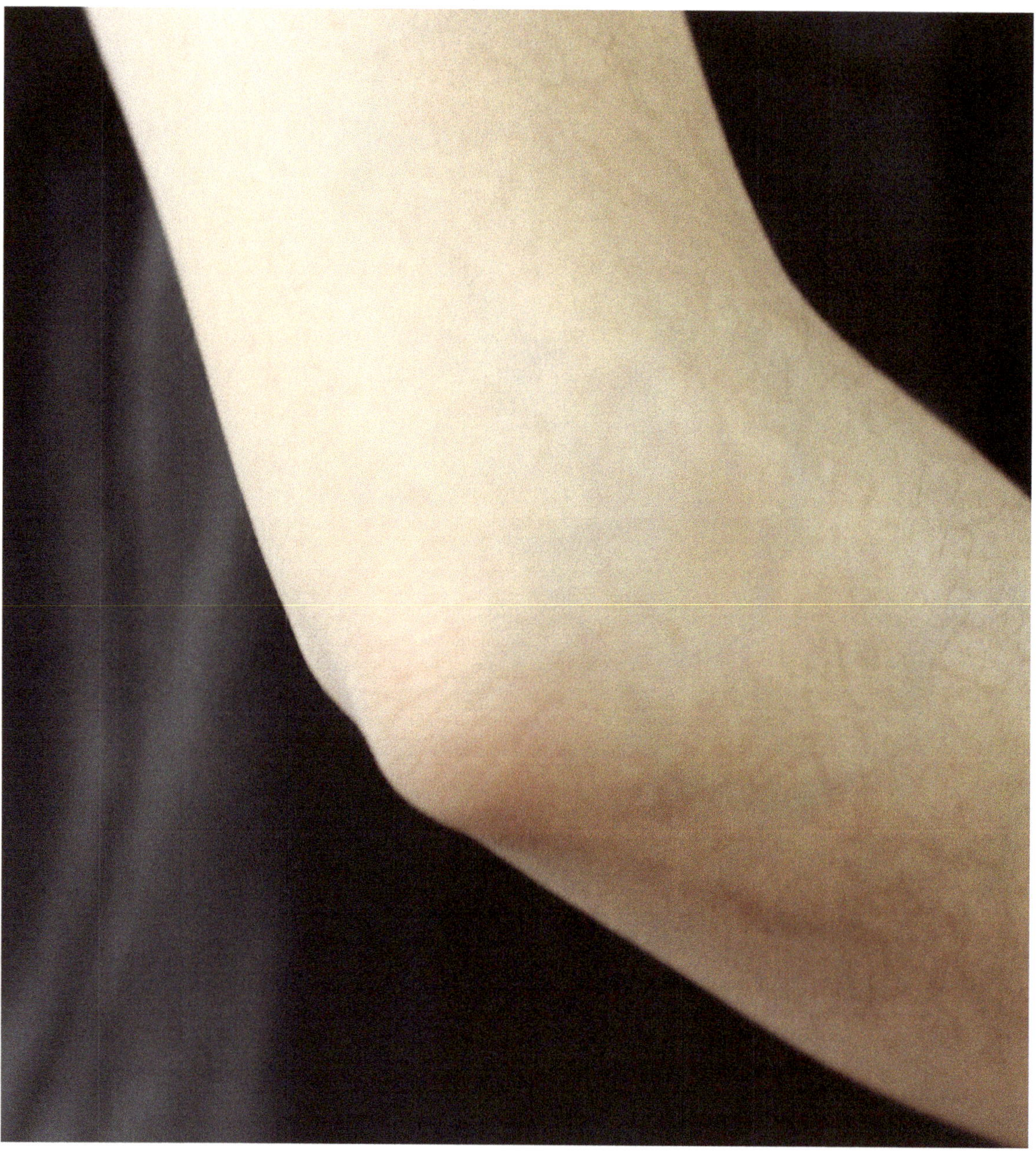

Now try drawing the elbow yourself without the grid.

Now that you have practiced different ways the elbow can express emotion and how light and shadow affect the eyes, try a couple of other perspectives. Pay attention to the shape of the elbow in different perspectives.

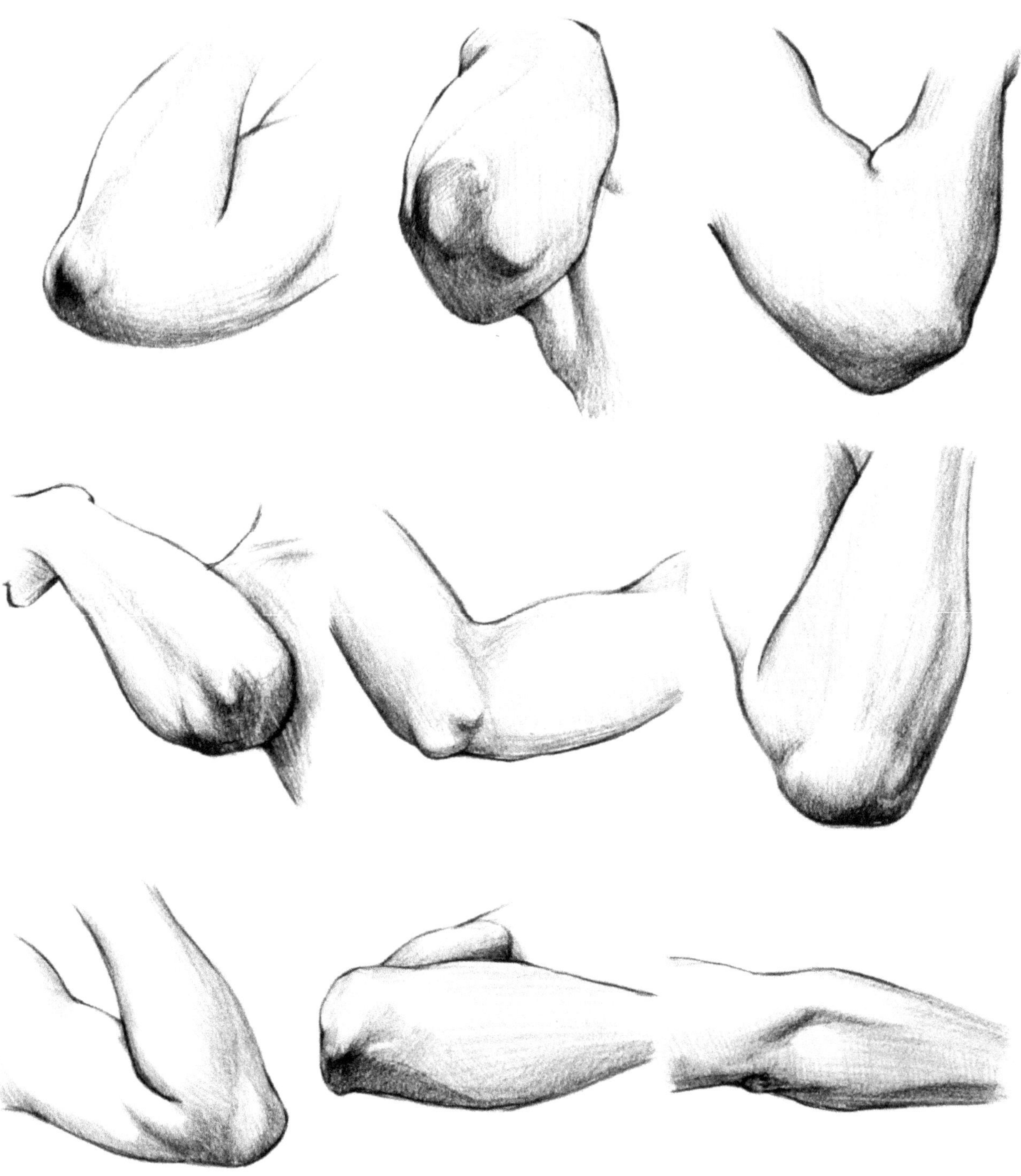

Now try drawing these general elbow positions yourself.

ABOUT OOGIE HAUS

Oogie Haus is an art foundation unique for its diverse artistic endeavors, including an emphasis in art education, art & design internship opportunities, and volunteer outreach programs. There have been several book publications as well, such as "Art College Admissions," an insightful guideline for students applying to art schools.

Besides being an educational resource, Oogie Haus functions dually as an art gallery and art dealership. Through its research, it seeks to contribute a bigger network for local and international artists simultaneously curating its unique voice in todays art world. For more information please visit www.oogiehaus.com

ABOUT THE AUTHOR

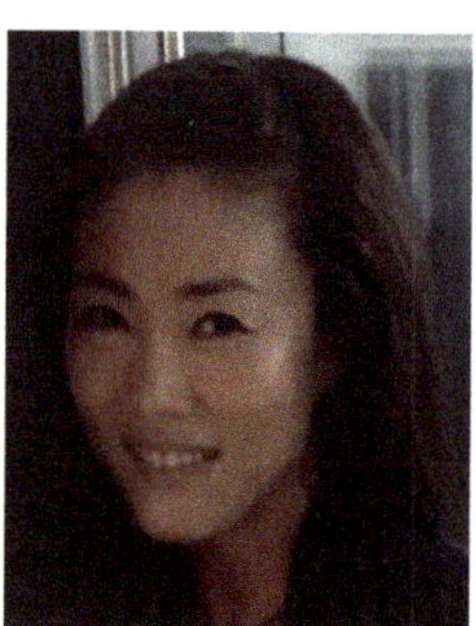

WOOK CHOI is an accomplished art dealer, education columnist, author, art educator, art gallerist, and art portfolio consultant who has guided over a thousand students to college admissions and scholarship success during the course of her 31-year teaching career.
She has received widespread recognition for her teaching methods from Mayor Michael Bloomberg; former First Lady Laura Bush; the New York Commissioner of Education, Richard P. Mills; US Congress member, Jerrold Nadler; the Alliance for Young Artists; YoungArts; and the Marie Walsh Sharpe Foundation. For more information, please visit www.wookchoi.com.

CHECK OUT SOME OF OUR OTHER BOOKS

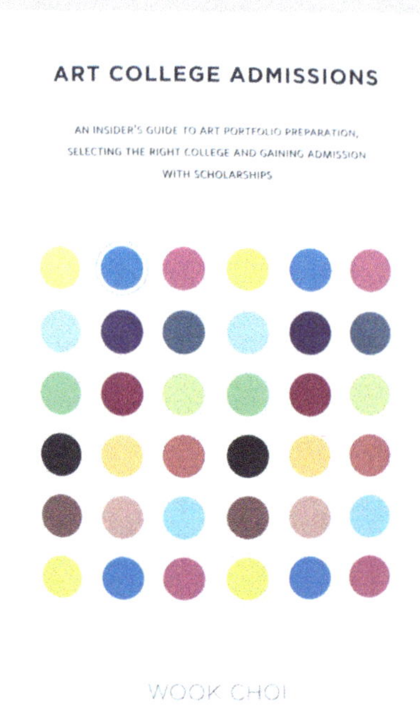

ART COLLEGE ADMISSIONS

An insider's guide to portfolio preparation, selecting the right college and gaining admission with scholarships.
In the first half of this book, you'll learn how vital a role art plays in the success of businesses today, what admissions committees at top art colleges really look for when deciding who to admit, and essential tips for developing award-winning art portfolio pieces. In the second half, you'll learn about the distinct advantages and histories of the most highly-ranked and popular art colleges in the Northeast, specific and actionable tips for getting into each school, and any changes these schools have made to their admissions criteria in recent years.

YOU CAN CONTINUE TO DEVELOP YOUR ARTISTIC SKILLS IN DIFFERENT MEDIA!

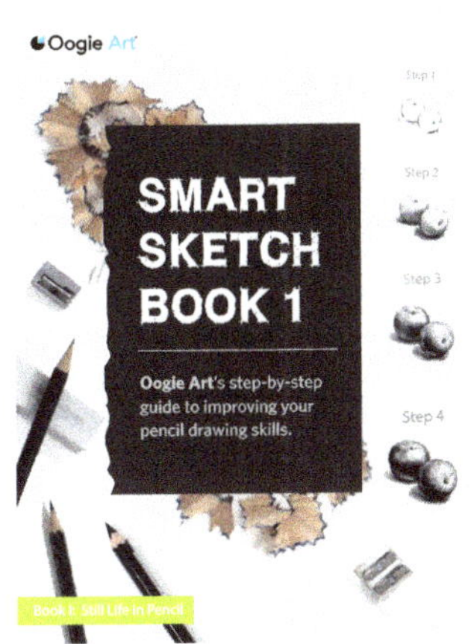

SMART SKETCHBOOK 1:
Still Life in Pencil

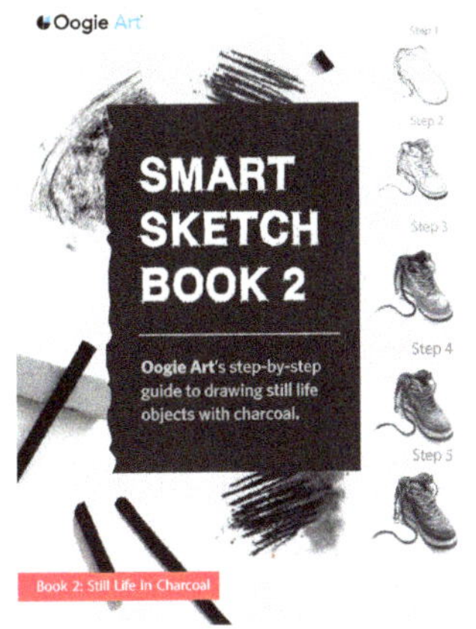

SMART SKETCHBOOK 2:
Still Life in Charcoal

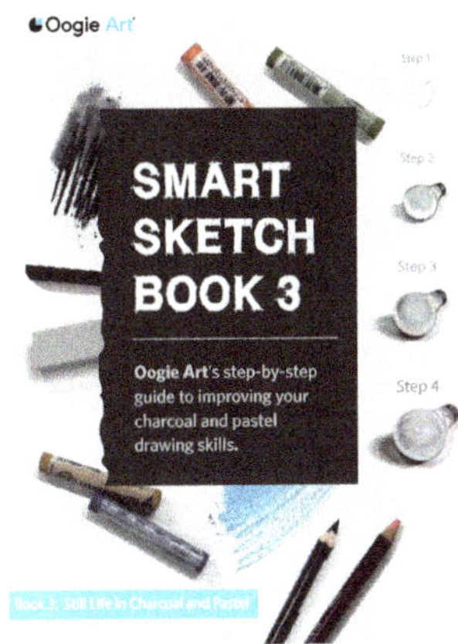

SMART SKETCHBOOK 3:
Still Life in Charcoal and Pastel

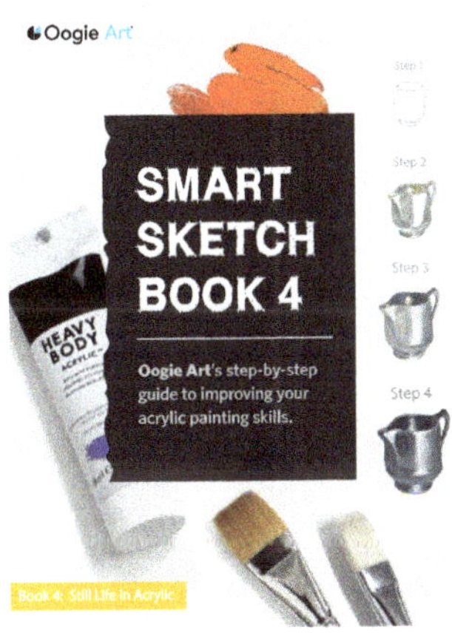

SMART SKETCHBOOK 4:
Still Life in Acrylic

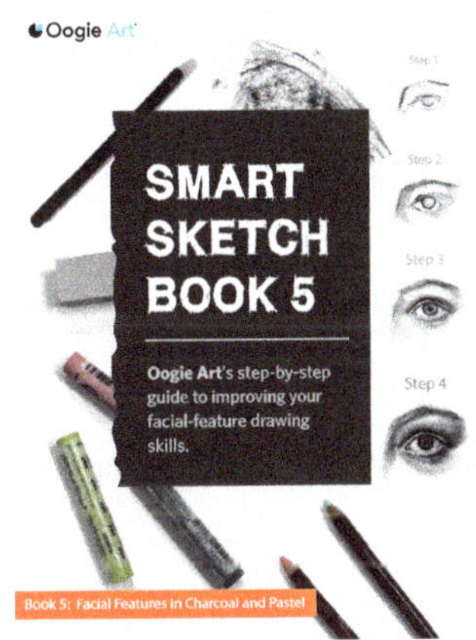

SMART SKETCHBOOK 5:
Facial Features in Charcoal and Pastel

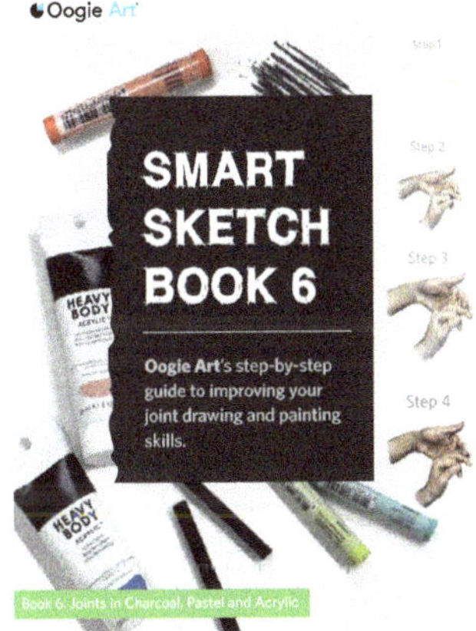

SMART SKETCHBOOK 6:
Joints in Charcoal, Pastel and Acrylic

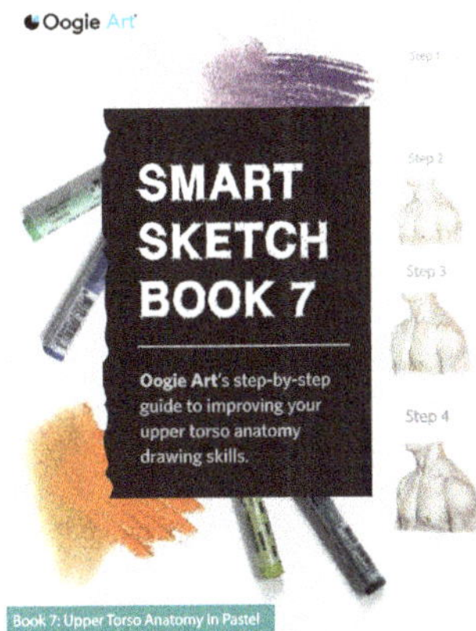

SMART SKETCHBOOK 7:
Upper Torso Anatomy in Pastel

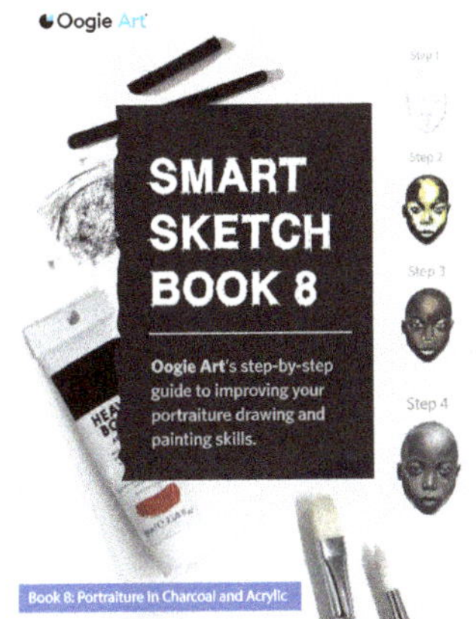

SMART SKETCHBOOK 8:
Portraiture in Charcoal and Acrylic

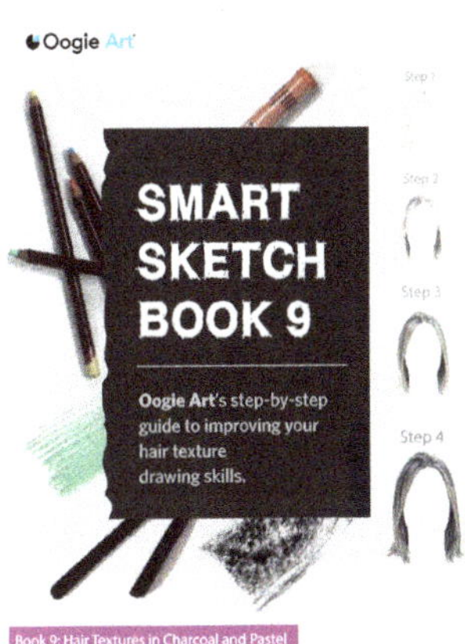

SMART SKETCHBOOK 9:
Hair Textures in Charcoal and Pastel

www.ingramcontent.com/pod-product-compliance
Ingram Content Group UK Ltd.
Pitfield, Milton Keynes, MK11 3LW, UK
UKHW062009290726
14090UKWH00022B/1477